GREAT WALKS

IRELAND

GREAT WALKS

IRELAND

DAVID HERMAN
Photography by Michael J. Stead

WARD LOCK

AUTHOR'S
ACKNOWLEDGEMENTS

I would like to thank the following most sincerely for their generous help in researching and editing this book. Any remaining errors in content are of course my own responsibility.

To Catherine Coxon and Mark Hennessy for checking my facts on the *clachan* system and early settlement patterns; to Dawson Stelfox for information on Cecil Newman and the hydro-electric scheme at Lough Belshade; to Graham Seymour and James McEvoy of the Northern Ireland Department of the Environment for details of right-of-way legislation in Northern Ireland; to Jimmy Murphy of Cospoir for information on Long Distance Routes; to Paddy Prendergast of the Ordnance Survey and Maurice Sheehy of Ventry for information on the tracks of Mount Eagle; to Sylvia and Victor Morrow who calmed my rising panic when faced with the Beenkeragh Ridge (it didn't turn out to be so terrifying!); and to Mark Herman who edited the 'semi-final' manuscript.

Lastly (and primarily) to my wife Mairin Geraty who pondered nearly every word in the manuscript and who walked nearly every mile of the routes with me.

First published in Great Britain in 1991
by Ward Lock Limited, Villiers House, 41/47 Strand,
London WC2N 5JE, England
A Cassell Imprint

© David Herman 1991

Text filmset by August Filmsetting, Haydock, St Helens

Printed and bound in Spain
by Artes Graficas Toleda S.A
D.L. TO: 1344–1991.

British Library Cataloguing in Publication Data
is available upon application to the British Library

ISBN 0 7063 6866 5

CONTENTS

Acknowledgement

Introduction   6

THE FACE OF IRELAND   8

An overview of the mountains   10
Mountain building: a clash of plates   13
Man and the Uplands   14
The hill lands today — and tomorrow?   16
The twilight of the Gaelic language   19

Introduction to the route descriptions   21

SELECTED WALKS IN THE EAST   25

Introduction   25

1. Easy Routes
1. The Cloghoge Valley   27
2. Canals of Kildare   32

2. Moderate Routes
3. Corries of the Comeraghs   36
4. The Lugduffs   40
5. Slieve Bearnagh   45

3. More Strenuous Routes
6. Galtymore   51
7. Traverse of the Mournes   54

4. Very Strenuous Route
8. Lugnaquillia and the Glen of Imaal   58

SELECTED WALKS IN THE NORTH-WEST   64

Introduction   64

1. Easy Route
9. Glenveagh   66

2. Moderate Routes
10. Slieve Snaght   70
11. Horn Head   74
12. Ben Bulbin   78
13. The Poisoned Glen Horseshoe   82

3. More Strenuous Route
14. The Blue Stacks   86

4. Very Strenuous Route
15. Errigal to Muckish   91

SELECTED WALKS IN THE WEST   96

Introduction   96

1. Easy Routes
16. Killary Harbour   98
17. Achill Head   104

2. Moderate Routes
18. The Benchoonas   108
19. The Burren   113

3. More Strenuous Routes
20. Central Maamturks   116
21. Mweelrea   121

4. Very Strenuous Route
22. The Glencoaghan Horseshoe   126

SELECTED WALKS IN THE SOUTH-WEST   132

Introduction   132

2. Moderate Routes
23. Mount Eagle   135
24. Gougane Barra   138
25. Bennaunmore   142
26. Cummeengeera Horseshoe   146
27. Mullaghanattin   151

3. More Strenuous Routes
28. Trails Around Killarney   154
29. The Coomloughra Horseshoe   160

4. Very Strenuous Route
30. Brandon   165

APPENDICES   170

Access and Rights-of-Way for the Walker   170
Safety   171
Giving a Grid Reference   172
Maps for the Walker   172
Addresses of Useful Organizations   174
Index   175

INTRODUCTION

Though it is a matter of supreme indifference to the rest of mankind, I have to declare that I really enjoyed 1990. Late in the previous year I had taken early retirement and almost immediately, received the offer to write this book — an offer I not only *could* not, but one that I certainly *would* not refuse under nearly any conceivable circumstance.

I have been wandering Ireland's mountains for 25 years, starting with my home base of Wicklow and gradually extending to nearly all the mountains of Ireland — and yes, there are still a few minor ranges in Ireland that I have not yet climbed. My expeditions have taken me farther afield, to Britain, the Alps, Malawi and the Himalayas. While these trips have been memorable and have provided a context for my own country, I still return to Ireland happy in the chauvinistic and irrational belief that they are the best and most rewarding mountains in the world.

To return to the present: the offer to write this book gave me the opportunity to do what I enjoy most, and so it was that in the spring, early summer and autumn of 1990 (high summer was too hot and humid for walking) I and a small team consisting of my walking companion — a nurse, a manager of food and accommodation and a general factotum — in a word my wife Mairin, set out to explore Ireland's mountains. It was an instructive project. Walking the mountains in a haphazard manner over a number of years and usually on someone else's route is one thing; a programme over six months with the necessity to record, compare, contrast and evaluate quite another. It brought formerly vague impressions into sharp focus and, like the supposed effect of the imminence of execution, it concentrated the mind wonderfully.

You may be interested in how I went about choosing routes in an area as large and diverse as Ireland. The first constraint was of course the limited number of routes I was allowed. I have already written guide books containing 60 or so different routes in *one* Irish mountain range so I quickly realized that to achieve 30 routes for the entire country, a ruthless, nay brutal, discarding of potentially attractive routes would be the order of the day. After that I decided that variety, a very easy objective in Ireland, would be my watchword.

I applied the rule of variety *within* each region so that the walker would explore a wide range of terrains, and also *within* the walks so that he would not be invited to walk a route of unchanging scenery. Even walking in superb country can eventually become a trudge along a conveyor belt running in reverse if the views are unvarying.

I also decided to limit the number of routes entailing a second car or a well-disposed, non-walking driver willing to pick up the walkers at the end. Where I have chosen such A to B routes, I have made the starting and finishing points either so close together that they are within walking distance for those who cannot organize a car at the finish, or so far apart that the walkers will have a sense of having made a long, hopefully satisfying traverse at the end of the day.

I am acutely aware that my 30 routes are unlikely to be those favoured by everyone or, worse still, *anyone* familiar with Ireland. The end result is a mixture: some easy strolls, some tough walks, some well-known classics, some virtually unknown territory. I have also omitted a few popular routes, omissions which I explain at appropriate points in the text. In spite of what may be considered a slightly idiosyncratic choice I hope that you, the reader and potential walker, will get more than a few good walks from my selection. As has been said before in another context: if only one person gets only one enjoyable walk from this book — I shall be bitterly disappointed!

One problem that I expected to come up against was the daunting task of attempting to describe the beauty and atmosphere of Ireland's mountain ranges. I need not have worried. Michael J. Stead in the magnificent photographs which embellish this book has done the job far, far better than my mere words. If these photographs don't entice you to don your walking boots and set off forthwith, nothing will.

'Warts and all' tends to be my approach, even though my conclusion after the intense programme of walking is that Ireland's mountains are as lovely as I ever thought they were and even more varied. With this in mind, I hope that readers will take the occasional criticism as a counterbalance to the considerable praise and appreciation which these pages contain. At a basic level, criticism has the virtue of making praise credible. I also feel it is important for visitors to realize that Ireland is 'different', and that these differences may express themselves in ways which they might occasionally find infuriating rather than engaging. If you know beforehand about the few problems that may occur, you will be far better prepared to take them in your stride. Please don't be put off by them.

I began by saying how much I enjoyed 1990. It is my sincere wish that when you come to Ireland you too will get at least as much pleasure and enjoyment in walking our mountains as I did in the happy year I spent exploring them.

D.H.

THE FACE OF IRELAND

INTRODUCTION

In extending a cordial invitation not only to peruse this book, but also to come to Ireland and explore the mountains, it is necessary to face honestly the fundamental question: why come to Ireland; and, if you do come, why make the additional effort of climbing the mountains?

Perhaps the most evident quality of Irish mountains is their small scale. They lack the soaring and overpowering majesty and vast panoramas of Alpine peaks — but are no whit inferior on that account. What they have is a human scale, a landscape in which a changing scene unfolds round every corner, a terrain in which only modest efforts are needed to achieve worthy peaks. It is not a country for the hardened and super-fit only: anyone who is moderately fit can experience and enjoy it. This is not to claim that Irish mountains are the only ones in the world to have a human scale. Of course, this is not true. Visitors from Britain, to cite the nearest example, can validly make exactly the same claim. So what are the qualities that make Irish mountains unique, and that will attract hillwalkers to this somewhat remote island?

Perhaps Ireland's unique attraction for the hillwalker lies in two characteristics that at first glance appear to be incompatible. These are remoteness and accessibility, and since they appear to be mutually exclusive it is necessary to consider them in conjunction.

Let us take remoteness first. Primarily and obviously, Ireland's mountains are by and large unfrequented. It is quite possible to walk for hours in many Irish ranges without encountering a single soul. In the Alps the hillwalker of average ability can slog upwards for hours to be greeted at his highest goal by a restaurant whose coffee-sipping patrons feel entitled to cast disparaging glances at his honorably dishevelled figure. In the Lake District and parts of Wales there are usually other hillwalkers around, many in large groups. Of course you cannot grudge their presence, any more than they can afford to grudge yours. Nevertheless, large numbers do significantly detract from the remoteness of mountain areas. How refreshing, therefore, to roam hills where the only human contact in a day of walking may be a solitary farmer checking his flock.

Remoteness also manifests itself in an absence of trails and paths through the mountains. Trails and paths are at once facilitating and restricting — facilitating because they allow walkers to enter territory into which they might not otherwise safely venture, restricting because they do not encourage exploration. The lifeline of a path is difficult to forsake once it is grasped. Ireland — and there are of course exceptions to this statement — has mountains that are without paths, without trails, without cairns except on the summits. This is not to say that there are *no* paths anywhere: an excellent system of Long Distance Routes girdles, but in general does not encroach upon, the mountains.

There is, however, a down-side to remoteness; it puts greater responsibility on the individual walker. With the knowledge that he is likely to have no ready help and be far from a mountain rescue service in the case of an accident, the ability to use a map and compass becomes a necessity rather than a luxury. A walker might think twice before venturing into remote mountains. It is not justifiable to make too much of this; after all, every hill-walker worth his salt should be able to use a map and compass. In Ireland, quite simply, there will be more occasions when it will be necessary, in spite of the accurate and detailed route descriptions in this book!

The other quality which, when taken together with remoteness, constitutes the unique attraction of Irish mountains is accessibility. No point in Ireland is more than 5 miles (8 km) from a motorable road. This bland statement needs a slight qualification: what with potholes, bumps, bends and rough surfaces, some overseas motorists might ruefully conclude that some are *not* motorable. (This comment emphatically does not apply to Northern Ireland's excellent road network.) Providentially the layout of Ireland's small discrete mountain ranges means that even if the road is diabolical, the motorist does not have to endure it for a long distance. Any peak can be climbed in a single day from a comfortable base; many fine circuits, some described in the course of these pages, can be walked without recourse to rough camping. No need, therefore, for long, hard expeditions or bruising backpacking trips (although there are many opportunities for these). To summarize: in Ireland there are mountains that are easy to reach and explore, but which are nevertheless unfrequented and possess a remote and wild atmosphere. Where else does such a fortuitous combination occur?

Lastly, perhaps mention should be made of one unique though blindingly evident characteristic of Ireland: it is the only country inhabited mainly by Irish people! Like them or loathe them, the Irish and particularly Irish country people, are a race of individuals, of characters in a western world that is becoming as bland and uniform as sliced bread. Praise their religious devotion or deride their religious formalism, admire their strong patriotism or deplore their unthinking nationalism, the Irish, North and South, are a race of individuals, not ciphers. Yet, whatever their differences, most Irish people — and especially Irish country people — share this much: they are kind, inquisitive in a friendly, non-threatening way, polite, generous and warm-hearted. This is something worth bearing in mind given the tragic events on this island in the last two decades.

AN OVERVIEW OF THE MOUNTAINS

That omniscient entity, 'every schoolboy' of Victorian fame, was undoubtedly aware that Ireland is shaped like a saucer, the higher land round the coast, the lowlands in the centre. Though it is a very rough saucer, there is more than an element of truth in the old cliché. The main mountain ranges *are*, broadly speaking, grouped near the coast, particularly the Atlantic coast, and the central area is an undulating plain which reaches the sea only in the 50-mile (80 km) stretch from Dublin to Dundalk.

In a purely statistical sense Ireland is not mountainous: only 5 per cent of the total area is over 1000 ft (305 m), and a mere 0.25 per cent over 2000 ft (610 m). Nor are the mountains high; there is only a handful of Munros (strictly, mountains in Scotland over 3000 ft (914 m), but a term used for those in other areas), and of these but two peaks reach the 1000 m contour. But statistics can be misleading. Over large areas of the country mountain ranges rear up impressively to belie their modest heights, dominating the plains in soft purple and blue hues in summer, gleaming with snowcaps in winter, disappearing in murky gloom and dull grey clouds at any time of year.

To some extent the mountains of Atlantic Ireland from Donegal in the north, through Mayo, Galway and Clare and reaching down to Kerry in the south have, whatever their many individual differences, two major features in common. Firstly, the sea. The sea, whether it is the wild Atlantic, the long, straight, drowned river valleys of the south-west, or the inlets, bays and fiords further north, is never far away. It is often within sight from the hills, and sometimes even from lower ground.

Secondly, and even more apparent than the sea is the setting of the mountains of Atlantic Ireland, a rugged environment in which human habitation clings precariously to the narrow strip between ocean on one side and mountain and bog on the other. Drive west from Oughterard in Galway or from Tralee in Kerry, and the ambience changes swiftly and perceptibly. The ruins of a wayside cottage, the whiff of turf fires and the donkeys grazing by the road — all hackneyed tourist clichés — clearly betoken a land in which man struggles to retain a precarious foothold in an unpromising terrain dominated by nature. In this terrain the mountains are a major and pervasive element.

The mountains of the rest of the country consist mainly of a group of ranges in the south and south-east and the Mournes in Northern Ireland. The typical east-west folds of the mountains of Munster in the south, of which the Galtees and the Comeraghs are the chief, give way further north to the granitic north-east to south-west trend of the Mournes and the Wicklow Mountains. The latter comprise the largest stretch of upland in Ireland with the highest peak outside Kerry.

The Mournes, Co. Down

These mountains are nearly as high as the mountains of the Atlantic coast and many are just as rugged. What these mountains have in common is that they rise, not from a bleak environment like that to the west, but from rich agricultural land, from pastoral fields and arable land or even from the outskirts of towns and villages. Similarly, though all except the Galtees are considered to be coastal ranges, they rise not from the wild Atlantic but from the narrow Irish Sea, the North Channel and St George's Channel. Though the mountains of the east lack only a little of the grandeur and ruggedness of the mountains of Atlantic Ireland, they do lack much of its harsh and splendid ambience.

Cummeengeera, Co. Kerry

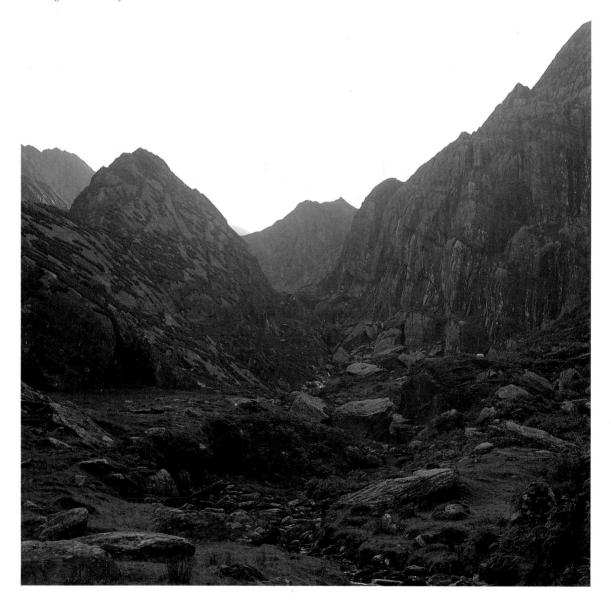

MOUNTAIN BUILDING: A CLASH OF PLATES

Mountain building occurs when tectonic plates, which are enormous segments of the earth's crust, collide. Two such collisions had repercussions in the area which is now Ireland, and between them they account for the general orientation and to some extent the type of rock that is exposed on the hills today. These two periods are termed the Caledonian and the Armorican.

The Caledonian episode of mountain building occurred over a long period which ended about 450 million years ago. This episode was not confined to Ireland; most of the mountains of Scotland were formed in the same period, and indeed give their name to the whole phenomenon. The collision of the plates resulted in compression wrinkles running in a north-east to south-west line over most of the country, with the significant exception of the south-west corner. Not only were mountain folds raised; the existing rock was metamorphozed by the intense heat and pressure of the collision into hard quartzites, schists and marbles.

The mountains of the south-west — that is, the mountains of Kerry, the Galtees and other ranges along or south of this line — were oriented into their now characteristic east-west line much later, about 340 to 280 million years ago in a collision of two plates to the south of Ireland. This, the Armorican mountain building episode, also affected the hills of South Wales and Devon. Once again, the existing rocks were metamorphozed.

In the many millions of years since these two mountain building episodes, the areas of the present hills have been submerged under the sea and subsequently uplifted. They have since been greatly weathered, the extent of which depends on what rock is exposed to the elements. Thus limestone, a soft rock, eroded away from the mountains of Kerry, leaving the hard underlying sandstone exposed; and the granite, which is a hard rock but one susceptible to chemical attack, weathered into the characteristic, gentle domes of the Wicklow Mountains.

By contrast, the Ice Age began in Ireland only a few hundred thousand years ago and ended a mere 10,000 years ago, an eyeblink in geological terms. Although a comparatively minor event, the Ice Age, because it is so recent, has left a lasting imprint on the mountain landscape, transforming what might otherwise be dull upland plateaux into sharp cliff-bound peaks. Glaciers, which at one stage or another affected the entire island except the highest peaks of the south, gouged out the corries from the sides of mountains and deepened shallow V-shaped valleys into deep U-shaped ones. These and other effects are discussed in more detail where glacial features are encountered on the routes themselves.

MAN AND THE UPLANDS

The 4500 years that elapsed between the end of the Ice Age and the first arrival of man are a period of conjecture, and more conjectural still for the mountain areas. We can, however, say with some certainty that the retreat of the ice left a tundra-like landscape, particularly on the uplands. However, as a milder climate developed, great forests — both deciduous and coniferous — advanced over the lowlands and spread less surely onto the uplands where the conifers, which are less demanding, tended to predominate.

This was the terrain into which the first settlers ventured about 5500 years ago, at a time when the climatic optimum for the forests was already over, with the coming of a wetter, colder climate more akin to our own. Assisted by the tentative clearances for agriculture made by succeeding generations of settlers, this deterioration in climate caused the beginnings of the demise of the great forests.

From about 2000 BC the upland forests — and they grew at altitudes of 2000 ft (610 m), maybe higher — began to succumb to blanket bog (so called because it 'blankets' the existing terrain) just as the trees of the lowlands were yielding to raised bog. However, bogs — blanket and raised — have one useful characteristic which enables scientists to find out about this remote period of pre-history. By sinking tubes into the bog and removing cores from different depths, and analyzing the pollen count found in them, scientists can establish the vegetational history of the area. The bog is almost literally a history book. This technique together with carbon-dating, by which the age of a specimen can be determined, tells us much of what we now know about pre-history.

Today, in many places in the uplands the walker will come across evidence of these ancient forests in the form of tree stumps in the lower layers of the now-decaying bog. This so-called 'bog oak' (it is more likely to be pine) had been smothered by the encroaching bog and preserved in its anaerobic (oxygen-free) environment. As we shall see, the bogland is now in turn coming under attack and so the tree stumps are being exposed.

The demise of the great forests, discontinuous though inexorable, went on throughout the Christian era, though climate changes caused retreats as well as advances in the extent of blanket bog on the uplands. However, humans, in increasing numbers and with increasingly sophisticated techniques, became the final arbiters of vegetational history on both upland and lowland.

To examine the effects of human habitation it is interesting to go back in time to look at the settlement pattern that developed all over the country, but especially in the less fertile west and north. The original Celtic settlements seemed to have been ring-forts, rough circular enclosures of earth surrounding huts belonging to a group of related families. From this tradition the *clachan* and the related farming system, *rundale*, developed in the Middle Ages. The *clachan* was a cluster of small farm-houses owned by a group of blood-related families. It was surrounded by an arable open-field. The field was divided into narrow strips, each strip held by a family. In some areas the strips were not held permanently, but by each family in turn. Further out were pastures, meadows, mountain land and bog, all held in common. At the beginning of summer cattle were moved with their herders into the mountain pastures to allow crops to grow untrampled; this was the booley tradition that survived vestigially on Achill Island as late as the 1950s. Traces of old booley dwellings are frequently encountered in the mountains, as well as ringforts and the occasional *clachan* lower down, the latter rarely easily recognizable especially since not all clusters of ruined houses are *clachans*.

The old, sad story of the Norman invasion of Ireland in the twelfth century and the Tudor plantations in the seventeenth, the latter resulting in the ebb and flow of war and destruction which Ireland suffered for so long thereafter, is sufficiently known in broad outline that we need not dwell on it. Suffice to say that most of the native Irish landowners were eventually driven to the poorer lands of the west and into the uplands. Indeed, the mountains provided the last refuge for rebels even as late as the end of the eighteenth century.

The *rundale* system existed into the time of a great population explosion that began about 1750 and ended in disaster less than 100 years later, a disaster which destroyed the system, the remaining remnants of forest and much else besides. The population rise was facilitated by the potato, a vegetable peculiarly suited to Ireland, even in the ill-drained mountainous west. It provided a deadeningly monotonous but nourishing diet to an increasing, and increasingly impoverished population. As numbers rose, more and more marginal land (even booley land) was turned over to potato growing, thus putting severe pressure on the traditional *rundale* system, which depended on the rotation of crops. The increasing numbers also meant that *rundale* became an encumbrance because of endless sub-division. Contemporary literature quotes a story of a holding of 4 acres (1.6 hectares) spread over 1 mile (1.6 km); and one of a horse shared by three men, each of whom claimed a leg so leaving the fourth hoof unshod. In circumstances as bizarre as these it is little wonder that many landlords encouraged the re-organization of their land.

The effect of land pressure was also felt in the forests. The remaining forests, already depleted over preceding centuries for fuel and to deprive rebels of shelter, were doomed. Except for the remnants behind the high walls of the landlords' demesnes, all that was left was ruthlessly stripped to provide additional land for potatoes and for fuel. But even such panic measures could not stave off disaster. The Great Famine struck in 1844 and was caused by the complete failure of the potato crop. It lasted five terrible years. Out of a population of $8\frac{1}{2}$ millions, the Famine left 1 million dead and caused another million to flee the country. The de-population was particularly acute in the mountain areas of the south and west. Today, though again uncertainly increasing, the total population of the whole island is still only 5 million.

The results of the Famine linger on today or have only recently abated: socially in continuing emigration and in late marriages or celibacy, physically in ruined houses and cottages and in the traces of former tillage ridges climbing up the hillsides, now being invaded by bracken. You will find many tragic reminders of this sea-change in the environmental (and social) history as you walk the mountains.

The Famine also resulted in a change in the settlement pattern and eventually the ownership of both uplands and lowlands. The *rundale* system, already seriously weakened before the Famine, gave way to tenant-occupiers and later to owner-farmers. Houses are now strung out along roads with individually owned, enclosed fields running up towards the hills. Above these fields is mountain land held in common, with each of a group of farmers entitled to run a fixed number of sheep on it. The state has planted new forests, but these can hardly be said to replace the old deciduous woods, being all too often monotonous swathes of conifers planted on marginal land far into the hills. The remnants of the old woods can be seen in Killarney (County Kerry) and Glendalough (County Wicklow), though even these may not be primeval forests but secondary woodland of a later age.

THE HILL LANDS TODAY — AND TOMORROW?

Let us now look at the present picture in more detail, and in doing so examine how the changes are affecting, and probably will increasingly in the future affect, the hillwalker. Unless otherwise indicated the conditions described are relevant to the Republic of Ireland, not Northern Ireland, though conditions there do not differ all that radically.

First, let us examine the effect that a comparatively recent decision taken in faraway Brussels has had on the Irish mountains.

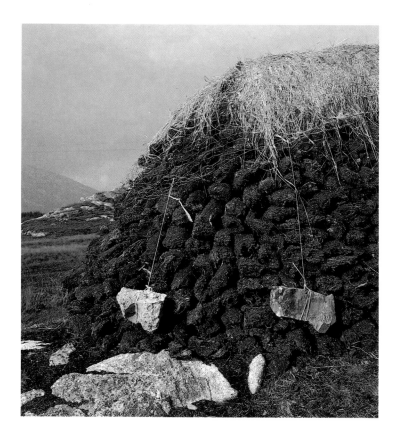

A peat stack

European Commission grants for sheep have greatly contributed to at least the impairment of the blanket bog in many areas, particularly in the west. This was perhaps initiated by climatic changes, but over-grazing by too many grant-aided sheep has certainly accelerated it. With the vegetation cover depleted, fissures occur in the bog, particularly in the more level stretches, eventually leaving peat hags (mounds of vegetated bogland). The penultimate stage in the destruction of the bog is the collapse of the hags into a thin layer of black mud. And finally, when even this is washed away, all that is left is bare rock.

To meet the threat of over-grazing, some commonages are being divided up into individual plots complete with the fencing in of each plot and an 'agricultural' road, the former an all-too-effective barrier to access, the latter an eyesore visible for miles around. For the hillwalker, and this is in the context of the Republic's antiquated laws on rights-of-way, commonage land has the great advantage that once gained, the walker is most unlikely to be challenged. Though a minor threat at present, the division of commonage might close off more and more areas to the walker.

Some of the divided plots might be given over to impenetrable forestry, also EC-aided, thus extending access difficulties for hillwalkers into private lands — difficulties that up to now have been almost exclusively confined to publicly-owned forested lands.

The encouragement of state forestry (now to be augmented by private) has been the policy of successive governments for 50 years. Though the first forests were planted with scant regard for the terrain, later ones are more sympathetic to it and have included amenity planting of deciduous trees, especially at their margins. In addition, as forests have grown to maturity they have been progressively opened to the public and provided with picnic sites, paths and trails. Whether this enlightened approach will survive under new 'hard-nosed' semi-state management (as opposed to the previous state control) remains to be seen.

Because of the poor right-of-way legislation in the Republic, forest tracks have served another useful purpose: Long Distance Routes, especially the first ones, have tended to be routed along them, thus avoiding private property. Appropriately, because of its more up-to-date legislation, Northern Ireland developed the first Long Distance Route in the island, the ambitious Ulster Way, which encircles the entire area. Northern Ireland also has a modest system of shorter right-of-way paths which the Republic as yet lacks.

The Republic, however, has no fewer than 20 Long Distance Routes, totalling 590 miles (950 km), ranging in length from a few miles to 135 miles (217 km). Some are waymarked, some not yet. The walks traverse all varieties of country — lots of forest, but also agricultural countryside, bogs, hills, river and canal banks. In general they do not venture over the tops, but instead skirt the mountains. An exception to this is the Wicklow Way, which rises to over 2000 ft (610 m), an aberration made before policy was finally decided. The Long Distance Routes of the Republic are not well depicted on the maps (except for part of the Western Way), mainly because maps on which they can be satisfactorily depicted do not yet exist. Details of all Long Distance Routes can be obtained from the addresses given in the Appendix.

Lastly, National Parks. These can hardly be considered a recent development since the first National Park was established as long ago as 1932. Fortunately the area under National Park control continues to expand, though at present it still constitutes less than a half of 1 per cent of the Republic's area. A pitiably small proportion indeed, but it does encompass some of the prime mountain landscapes. Six of the walks in this book are through or close to National Parks and the reason for this is not simply because of their presence, but more importantly because of their inherent beauty and attractiveness.

National Parks in Ireland differ fundamentally from those in England and Wales in that they are wholly state-owned (this is, incidentally, the internationally recognized norm). This means that they are devoted to the needs of visitors where this does not clash with conservation. Each National Park is well and sensitively managed with an interpretative centre, trails and informational material. Individual National Parks are described in more detail under the appropriate route description. Northern Ireland has no National Parks, but it does have Areas of Outstanding Natural Beauty (AONBs), which have the same standing as in the rest of the United Kingdom. One, which covers the entire area of the Mournes, Northern Ireland's most attractive mountain range, is of particular interest to walkers. While an AONB cannot provide as high a degree of protection as the Republic's National Parks, it does provide adequate protection at the same cost for a greater area.

The Twilight of the Gaelic Language

The Gaelic language (generally called 'Irish' in Ireland) was a major victim of the Famine of the 1840s, though already on the decline before that. Widely spoken in the western half of the country before the Famine, the cycle of emigration, exclusively to English-speaking countries, which that disaster set in train, resulted in English being seen as the language of economic advancement. The new state set up in 1921 has tried to reverse that trend, with a conspicuous lack of success in all but externals. It has been a costly policy with little of real value to show for it. What we have now are much of the outward paraphernalia of a Gaelic-speaking country (such as in signposting, names of government and semi-government agencies, etc.). What we don't have, except in some western seaboard areas, are living communities which actually speak Gaelic.

One of the Celtic group of languages, Gaelic is closely related to Scots-Gaelic and Manx, and less closely related to the other Celtic branch comprising Welsh, Breton and Cornish. The script was modernized in the 1950s and the artistic but technically troublesome old Gaelic script was dropped in favour of the present one, which is the same as English and other modern European scripts. This explains the ugly proliferation of the letter 'h' in the present standard script; it is a circumflex, not a letter, and cannot be neatly accommodated. Generally it softens the preceding consonant, though it sometimes has the effect of a literary black hole, swallowing it and leaving nothing to pronounce.

Irish shopfront

One field in which Gaelic has a direct impact on the visitor is in place-names, even if this impact is nothing more than the difficulty they present in pronunciation, a subject on which this book can offer only a little help where difficult words occur in the text. Nearly all place-names in Ireland are of Gaelic origin, particularly those of natural features, which are of special concern to the walker. Each name was once appropriate and meaningful to the Gaelic-speaking local people. When the English-speaking Ordnance Survey officials of the nineteenth century tried to give official place names for the new maps they were preparing, they had the obvious difficulty of writing down the unfamiliar sounds of a strange language. The resulting official names, which are still on the OS maps, are in many cases far from felicitous.

The Gaelic-speaking areas ('Gaeltachts') have now shrunk to a few margins on the western seaboard covering perhaps 10–20,000 people who habitually speak Gaelic, areas which providentially coincide with some of the best hillwalking country. The walker will therefore have a good chance of hearing, in its cultural setting, a language which had a rich literature and was already a millenium old when English was a primitive, emergent *patois*.

INTRODUCTION TO THE ROUTE DESCRIPTIONS

1. ACCESS

See page 170.
NB The representation in this book of a road, track or path is not evidence of the existence of a right-of-way.

2. ASCENT

The amount of climbing involved in each route has been estimated from the appropriate map and should be regarded as approximate only.

3. CAR-PARKS

Many routes start at a public car-park. For other routes places are indicated where a car can be parked by the wayside, but it must be done with care, as indiscriminate parking can be a great nuisance to local people.

4. INTERESTING FEATURES ON THE ROUTE

The best position for seeing these is indicated both in the route descriptions and on the maps by *(1)*, *(2)*, etc.

5. LENGTH

These are strictly 'map miles' estimated from the appropriate map; no attempt has been made to take into account any ascent or descent involved.

6. MAPS

The maps are drawn to a scale of approximately 1:25 000 or 1 : 50 000 and all names are as given on Ordnance Survey maps. Field boundaries in particular, which can be a mixture of hedge, fence and wall, should be taken as a 'best description'. The arrow on each map points to grid north. The scale of some small features has been slightly exaggerated for clarity.

A discrepancy has arisen between the OS imperial and metric maps. Mathematically-inclined readers armed with a calculator and much idle curiosity will have noticed that the imperial heights given in this book do not always correspond to the metric. The reason is that the heights are taken from the relevant metric and imperial maps and these do not exactly correspond, either because they are recorded on slightly different points or because of the higher accuracy of the metric.

SYMBOLS USED ON ROUTE MAPS

☐ Ruin   △ Summit

✗ Gate   Cliff

⊣⊢ Bridge

✚ Waterfall

····· No path

--- Path

=== Track

+++ Fence

■ Occupied building

π Stile

∞∞ Wall

▲ OS Obelisk

✚ Church

7. ROUTE DESCRIPTION

The letters 'L' and 'R' stand for left and right respectively. Where these are used for changes of direction they imply a turn of about 90° when facing in the direction of the walk. 'Half L' and 'half R' indicate a half-turn, i.e. approximately 45°.

8. STANDARD OF THE ROUTES

The briefest examination of the route descriptions that follow will show that the routes described cover an enormous range of both length and difficulty; the easiest can probably be undertaken by a family party at almost any time of the year whilst the hardest are only really suitable for experienced walkers who are both fit and well-equipped. Any walker therefore who is contemplating following a route should make sure before starting that it is within his or her ability.

It is not easy in practice, however, to give an accurate picture of the difficulty of any route, because it is dependent upon a number of factors and will in any case vary considerably from day to day with the weather. Any consideration of weather conditions must, of course, be left to the walker himself (but read the section on safety first). Apart from that, it is probably best to attempt an overall assessment of difficulty based upon the length, amount of ascent and descent, problems of route-finding and finally, upon the roughness of the terrain.

Each of the routes has therefore been given a grading based upon a consideration of these factors and represented by the bold numerals which precede each walk title. A general description of each grade follows:

Easy (1) Generally short walks (up to 5 miles, 8 km) usually over well-defined paths, with few problems of route-finding. Some climbing may be involved, but mostly over fairly gradual slopes with only short sections of more difficult ground.

Moderate (2) Rather longer walks (averaging about 8 miles, 13 km), but with sections where route-finding will be more difficult. Mountain summits may be reached with climbing over steeper and rougher ground.

More strenuous (3) Generally longer walks (averaging about 10 miles, 16 km), with prolonged spells of climbing. Some rough ground calling for good route-finding ability, perhaps with stretches of scrambling.

Very strenuous (4) Only for the few, involving long distances (up to 15 miles, 24 km), with a considerable amount of climbing, and perhaps stretches of scrambling.

The walks are arranged in order of increasing difficulty within each region.

A summary of each walk is given at the beginning of each route description with information on length, amount of climbing and any special difficulties, such as scrambling, that will be met along the way.

9. STARTING AND FINISHING POINTS

The location of each starting and finishing point is described along with its six-figure grid reference (see page 172).

10. TIME FOR COMPLETION

The usual method of estimating the length of time needed for a walk is by Naismith's Rule: 'For ordinary walking allow one hour for every 3 miles (5 km) and add one hour for every 2000 feet (600 m) of ascent; for backpacking with a heavy load allow one hour for every $2\frac{1}{2}$ miles (4 km) and one hour for every 1500 feet (450 m) of ascent.' However, for many this tends to be over-optimistic and it is better for each walker to form an assessment of his or her own performance over one or two walks. Naismith's Rule also makes no allowance for rest or food stops or for the influence of weather conditions.

11. GETTING TO THE STARTING POINT BY CAR

In Northern Ireland there should be no difficulty with road designations. The system used is identical to that used in the rest of the United Kingdom; that is, A, B and C designations. In the Republic of Ireland, however, an older system — T (for trunk) and L (for link) — is gradually being replaced by N (for national) and R (for regional) not necessarily respectively. While the change-over of the main roads to N is virtually complete, many secondary roads still have the old T or L designation. Worse still, some signposts indicate T or L and others R. For this reason, both designations have been used in the text where appropriate.

Many minor side-roads have no designations and may even be too modest to demand signposts. Nevertheless, they must be negotiated to reach the start of some of the walks in this book. To minimize the chance of getting lost in this confusing network, *precise* distances (to tenths of a mile or km) have been given, rather than the usual rougher approximations, where necessary. In these instances, it would be prudent to measure distances using the car's odometer. It is rather a nuisance, but better than the frustration of getting lost in a maze of minor roads.

Route locations

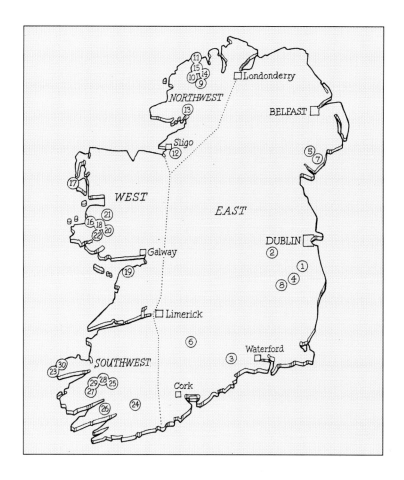

INTRODUCTION

Even a casual glance at the map of Ireland opposite will reveal that the East covers a large area, the whole island except the Atlantic seaboard, and that it contains a number of high mountain ranges, most of them in the south of the region. These ranges are not quite as wild and rugged as those further west, and they are surrounded by 'civilized' farmland, with towns and even cities close by, rather than by the inhospitable barren land of the west. Nor is the sea all that much in evidence; and when seen it is tame and placid. Access to these mountains by car, as might be expected, is comparatively easy though it is certainly not effort-less, as some of the complicated access directions will testify.

In this large and diverse area, two routes, or rather two moun-tains, stand out: the two Munros. Galtymore in the Galtees can be reached by a very easy but dull route from the south or a somewhat longer and much more attractive route encircling high corries on the northern side — an easy choice. Lugnaquillia in Wicklow can be climbed by several good routes. The circuit of the Glen of Imaal, the route to Lugnaquillia finally chosen, is strenuous, but the long, lingering high-level descent from the summit offers fine panoramic views.

The Glen of Imaal is on the quieter, western side of Wicklow (quieter, that is, when the Artillery Range in Imaal is not in use). The two other routes in Wicklow are on the sharper eastern side, the side of steep glacial valleys and corries etched into otherwise rounded mountains. The Cloghoge Valley is the loveliest in Wicklow, a superb blend of woodland, valley and lake, and a good area for visitors who have only a short time to spend around Dublin. The Lugduffs give a high-level panorama of much of the best of the range and as a bonus take in Glendalough, a valley justly famous for its monastic associations as well as for its wooded beauty. This whole area is now safe in the arms of the new Wicklow National Park, a most welcome development.

One cautionary and sad word on Wicklow before moving on. Do not leave valuables visible in your car; better, do not take valuables with you at all into any area of the Wicklow Mountains, remote or not. There have been too many cases of robbery in this region to risk it.

Glendalough, the mine workings

Between the Galtees and Wicklow lie the Comeraghs, probably the finest mountains in the area between these two major ranges. They are noted for their dramatic corries (and are notorious for their dull bleak uplands), one of which is probably rightly reputed to be the most dramatic corrie in Ireland. This has not been included in a route, because the route chosen, with three fine corries, gives better overall variety.

Far to the north in County Down are the Mournes, a small but rugged range of uneroded granite mountains, and with Connemara by far the best-mapped area in the entire island. Two routes are included here: a short but steep ascent to castellated Slieve Bearnagh; and a comparatively short traverse of the range (much longer traverses are possible). This traverse runs from the south at Slieve Binnian, where the Mournes really do 'sweep down to the sea', to the north at Newcastle, bypassing Slieve Donard, the highest peak in the range. *Bypassing* Slieve Donard? If you are keen on peak-bagging by all means climb it, but it is a smooth-sloped, dull, inverted pudding-bowl.

Lastly there is Robertstown, an area where the nearest hills are but a faint blue smudge on the eastern horizon. Its quiet backwaters, under-used canals and out-of-the-way villages are just the place to recuperate after the rigours of the mountains.

THE CLOGHOGE VALLEY

STARTING AND FINISHING POINT

On the L of the R759/L161 heading towards Sally Gap (172064). Take the R755/T61 and turn west (R coming from Dublin) onto the R759. Drive uphill for 2 miles (3.2 km) and park carefully on the side of the road near the set of large pillars on the L.

MAPS

OS 1:50 000 Sheet 56 and OS Wicklow District 1 inch to the mile are equally satisfactory.

LENGTH

4 miles (6.5 km) for the easy route; 6 miles (9.5 km) for the harder.

ASCENT

700 ft (210 m) for the easy route; 1700 ft (520 m) for the harder.

NOTE FOR DOG-OWNERS

Please do not take your pet on the longer route. It runs through a deer-rearing area and the land is poisoned.

Wicklow at its most scenic, a complex interplay of woodland and valley, lake and mountain, which is reminiscent of the less rugged, more scenic parts of England's Lake District. Two routes are described and both give marvellous views of Lough Tay, the rocky cliffs of Luggala which end in great boulders at its lakeshore and the partly wooded Cloghoge Valley (pronounced 'Clock-oge') which connects Tay to Lough Dan, the large secluded lake to the south. The *easy* route works its way diagonally down to the floor of the Cloghoge Valley and returns on a short but sharp ascent from near the shores of Lough Dan to attain a higher level than on the outward stretch. The *harder* route diverges from the easy one near Lough Dan, continues along the north shore of the lake, climbs rocky Knocknacloghoge and returns through a side valley to the road.

ROUTE DESCRIPTION (Map 1.1)

Go through the gates labelled 'Ballinrush' 70 yards (65 m) down-hill from the large pillars and on the same side *(1)*. The walk from here to Lough Dan is as navigationally simple as it is scenically delightful: a straightforward stroll along a track downhill or level almost all the way *(2)*. (You will realize that there is an unpleasant snag to a looped walk which starts innocently with a lot of downhill.) When private property in the form of a large forbid-ding gate blocks the way ahead turn R down a narrow path through an ancient wood to the bank of the Cloghoge River directly opposite a two-storey house — a lovely place for a bite to eat and a rest, the latter hard to justify. The two routes part ways here.

Easy route Return along the path to the main track. Turn L onto it and branch first R steeply uphill onto a green track just before the first holiday home. At the first ruin on the L, turn R again steeply uphill with forest on the R. Turn L at the first track (it plunges on the R into forest) and follow it across open coun-try, which gives marvellous views L across to the high peaks of the range.

When forest blocks the way ahead, turn R uphill on another track thus heading for a prominent gate on the skyline. Pass

Map1.1 : The Cloghoge Valley

through it, turn L and with forest on the L continue straight ahead through forest. Where a forest road sweeps in — and away — on the R, cross the fence L and follow the track all the way back to the road. Turn L and walk the few yards back to the starting point.

Lough Tay and Luggala cliffs

Harder route Wade across the river using a rough weir a little way down-stream of the two-storey house. Turn L and pick up a path which hugs the northern shore of Lough Dan. At the spit of silver sand, which marks the western end of the lough turn R steeply uphill avoiding the crags L on the climb. At the sudden easing of the slope, head for the L of the two rocky hillocks ahead, picking up a path that improves as it nears the summit of Knockacloghoge (1754 ft/534 m).

From the summit walk directly north over rough, heathery ground to cross the Cloghoge Brook, then turn R down-stream following the L-hand bank closely. At a delightful pool below a tiny waterfall, join a green track and follow it through a gate and thence down to a main track. Turn L here, cross a wide bridge and walk to tarmac at a farmhouse on the R. Continue uphill *(3)* to a hairpin bend *(4)* and beyond it take the steep incline to the road and the starting point.

1   *The Peregrine Falcon*

The peregrine falcon nests on the Luggala cliffs which can be seen from the start, but better from the end of the walk. A fast and strong flyer, it has fast wing-beats interrupted by occasional gliding. Its wing span is about 3 ft (0.9 m). The bird is rare in Ireland (and elsewhere) but its range is slowly spreading.

2   *Heather*

The heather moorlands here are a blaze of purple in August, when walking across them produces a cloud of pollen. This area is generally reputed to be the best-managed heather moorland in Wicklow.

3   *Luggala House*

The elegant house which is built on the northern shore of Lough Tay, but only whose grounds are visible on this steep ascent, is owned by a member of the Guinness family (of brewing fame). Many famous people have visited the house, including the philosopher Bertrand Russell, who was captivated by the scenery. He returned years later and could not find the spots from which he had previously so enjoyed the view. He concluded philosophically that one should not re-visit places which one enjoyed the first time round.

4   *Two Irish Miles*

A notice on the house on the L encouragingly (and a trifle whimsically) announces in archaic Irish lettering and in plain English that it is 2 Irish miles to Lough Dan. It does not say that an Irish mile is considerably longer than an English one. The distance is actually 2 *standard* miles because the notice exaggerates the Irish mileage — so we are back to square one! At this juncture you will probably be less concerned about that and more about the climb to the road and the car. For the record, the climb is 300 (English) ft (90 m).

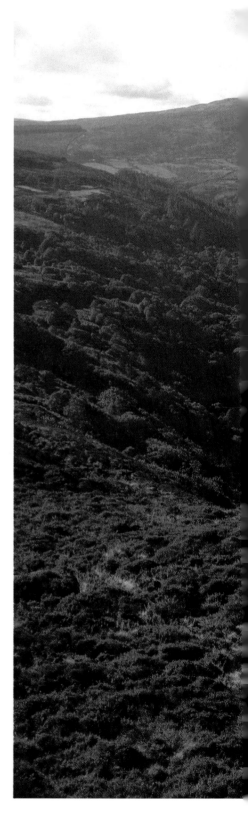

The Cloghoge Valley and Lough Dan

1·2

CANALS OF KILDARE

STARTING AND FINISHING
POINT
Robertstown, County Kildare
(790249). The village is situated
2 miles (3 km) south of the
R403/L2.
MAPS
The OS half-inch to the mile
Sheet 16 covers the area and
should be useful for the route to
Robertstown, but is on so small a
scale that it is of marginal use on
the walk. A leaflet with a sketch-
map covering all the Kildare canal
walks is available from Cospoir
— see Appendix.
LENGTH
8 miles (14 km)
ASCENT
Negligible.

Kildare is a flat inland county, and one not normally associated with walking. Nonetheless a system of walking routes has been laid out using as a centrepiece the canals that run through the county on their way from Dublin to the west and south-east. These routes traverse a country of pleasant villages and wet fields bounded by straggling unkempt hedges. Much of their length follows shallow, rarely used canals, arched by high humped-back bridges, whose banks support wildfowl, dragonflies and a variety of flowers. If you find that canal banks are a trifle tedious, take heart; the first stretch of canal bank is followed by sections of country road, forest and bog-land, which should refresh you before the final length of bank.

ROUTE DESCRIPTION (Map 1.2)

Following the gaudy signpost of the Kildare Way, cross the prominent Binn's Bridge in Robertstown *(1)* to reach the north side of the canal, thus leaving the main part of the village. Take the road beyond, continuing straight ahead along a narrow road beside the canal where the main road swings R. Just before Lowtown Marina, cross Fenton Bridge, pass around the Marina buildings *(2)* and cross the high footbridge beyond, where a signpost announces far-off and exotic destinations culminating in St Mullins 70 miles (112 km) away.

Turn L beyond the footbridge and walk along the towpath, passing one road-bridge (do *not* cross it). At the second bridge continue straight ahead onto a metalled road, pass Ballyteige Castle *(3)* and a lock; just beyond it, turn R onto a side-road, thus following the purple arrows of the 'Robertstown Local Walk' (you follow these to the end of the walk).

Take this narrow road, further on a rough farm road, initially through an area of scattered houses and later through a state forest, and past turfworkers' billets on the R *(4)* (both forest and billets appear by their unkempt and desolate appearances to be reverting to the gentle care of nature). Pass a turn on the L and at a T-junction turn L to pass to the R of the end of a raised bog *(5)*, with the cooling tower of Allenwood Power Station *(6)* ahead. At the next T-junction turn L onto the main road (not R as instinct for home would rightly suggest), and a few steps along turn R up a side-road, so reaching yet another stretch of canal. Turn R here to follow the towpath to the next bridge, Shee Bridge. Cross this bridge and continue along an overgrown towpath (now on the L bank) past Bond Bridge (do *not* cross this one), so reaching again the canal bank opposite Lowtown Marina. Return along the same side-road as the outward journey to reach Robertstown, turning R over Binn's Bridge to reach the village.

1 *Robertstown*
   The village owes its origin to the Grand Canal, work on which commenced in the middle of the eighteenth century. The large, imposing building in the village was originally a hotel owned by the Grand Canal Company, and is at present used by local tourist interests.

2 *Lowtown Marina*
   Lowtown lies at the junction of the Grand Canal and the Barrow Line, so canals radiate from here to Dublin, the River Shannon to the west, and the River Barrow to the south. From Lowtown water levels are controlled and the necessary paperwork to operate the canal is issued.

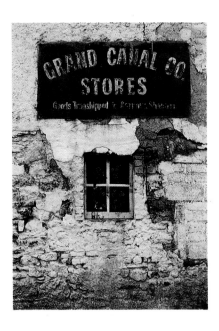

Sign on the old stores

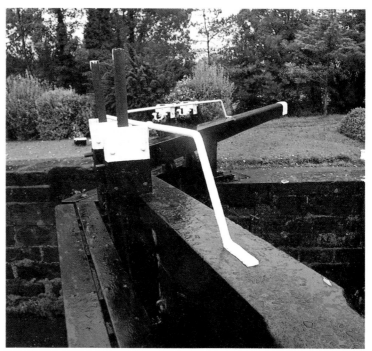

Left: *The bridge at Robertstown*   *Lock on Grand canal*

3 *Ballyteige Castle*
   This is a typical example of an Irish fortified house of the fourteenth to sixteenth centuries.

4 *Turfworkers' Billets*
   These were built during the fuel crisis of the 'Emergency', as World War II is still euphemistically called. They were intended as accommodation for workers harvesting peat from nearby bogs, but were never completed.

5 *Lullymore Bog*
   On the L is Lullymore Bog, a typical midlands raised bog, and part of what was the Great Bog of Allen before it succumbed to the cutting machinery for nearby peat-burning power stations. Its dome shape is caused by the accumulation of sphagnum, which is able to draw up water so that the bog surface can rise above the water-table.

6 *Allenwood Power Station*
   This power station burns sod peat from nearby bogs, Ireland being one of the very few countries in the world to have this type of fuel. The station is still open, having been given a reprieve from closure in the late 1980s.

CORRIES OF THE COMERAGHS

STARTING AND FINISHING POINT

In the townland of Lyre (264126). The starting point is difficult to find and requires careful attention to the following details. Take the R671/T27 (Dungarvan to Clonmel road) turning onto a minor road opposite Melody's Pub in Ballymacarbry village (the village is well signposted). Drive straight ahead for 2.1 miles (3.4 km), turning R uphill here. Turn L at an offset crossroads after another 0.5 miles (0.8 km), continue straight on past a R turn, the first on this stretch of road, after another 2.4 miles (3.8 km) and park considerately near a farmhouse on the L after another 0.3 miles (0.5 km). Have courage, most navigational problems are now behind — but take care not to get lost on the drive home.

MAP

OS half-inch to the mile Sheet 22. Luckily the route is such that it does not rely overheavily on the availability of a good map.

LENGTH

6½ miles (10.5 km)

ASCENT

1500 ft (460 m)

The central section of the Comeraghs (pronounced 'Come-err-ahs'), between the Sgilloge Gap and Coumfea 3 miles (5 km) to the south-west, is a dull, boggy plateau which greatly contrasts with the virtual ring of fine corries surrounding it. This walk takes in three of the corries, holding in all six lakes and several small lochans. Each corrie is backed by grassy slopes about 700 ft (210 m) high, here and there broken by protruding horizontal sandstone, while higher up the otherwise smooth skyline is disrupted by an occasional jagged pinnacle. In a surprisingly remote area this is a walk of constantly changing vistas and sudden revelations, with lakes cupped in deep hollows unexpectedly coming into view over heathery hillocks and rolling moorland.

ROUTE DESCRIPTION (Map 2.3)

With the farmhouse on your left walk along the road to the T-junction. Turn R and cross through a gate on the L 150 yards (135 m) along (a truly enormous flat boulder will be visible in the field beyond it). Walk downhill diagonally R towards the river (the Nier, pronounced and sometimes spelt *Nire*) and follow it upstream, crossing what appears to be a major tributary at a clump of trees, but is in fact the Nier itself. Continue straight ahead (thus *not* following the Nier) along an intermittent path beside the stream to walk to the R of a ruin that lies beyond the junction of two more tributaries. The trick here is to pick the correct tributary among the complex gathering of tributaries on the bleak moorland hereabouts: you may need to take a compass-bearing south-east on the lower Sgilloge Lough in order to find it. Walk on the R bank and note, for reassurance, the fence running parallel to the stream on the other bank.

A path develops along the bank of this tributary, and where the fence swings R across the path, look out R for the lower Sgilloge Lough, the least impressive of all the lakes on this route. Continue on a path along the near shore over hummocky ground to the upper Sgilloge Lough (*1*), which is surrounded by a great amphitheatre cut out of the cliffs with a narrow stream cascading down into its south-eastern corner — a good place for a rest.

The rule from here to the next corrie is to follow the contour of the hillside with the cliffs and high ground close on the L. At the upper Sgilloge Lough swing to the R to walk along the shore. Then walk to the so-far unvisited south side of the lower Sgilloge Lough and continue round the high, grassy ground on the L into the dull moorland at the lower edge of the next corrie, that holding Coumalocha (2). Once into the arms of the corrie swing

Access to start

R671

Melody's Pub, Ballymacarbry

2·1 miles

·5

2·4 miles

Lyre ·3

Map 2.3 : Corries of the Comeraghs

River Nier

Lyre

Ballymacarbry

STARTING AND FINISHING POINT

River Nier

300

450

600

① Sgilloge Loughs

N

② Coumalocha

Lough Coumfea

Coumfea

| 0 | | 1 | | 2 | | 3 Kilometres |

| 0 | | | 1 | | | 2 Miles |

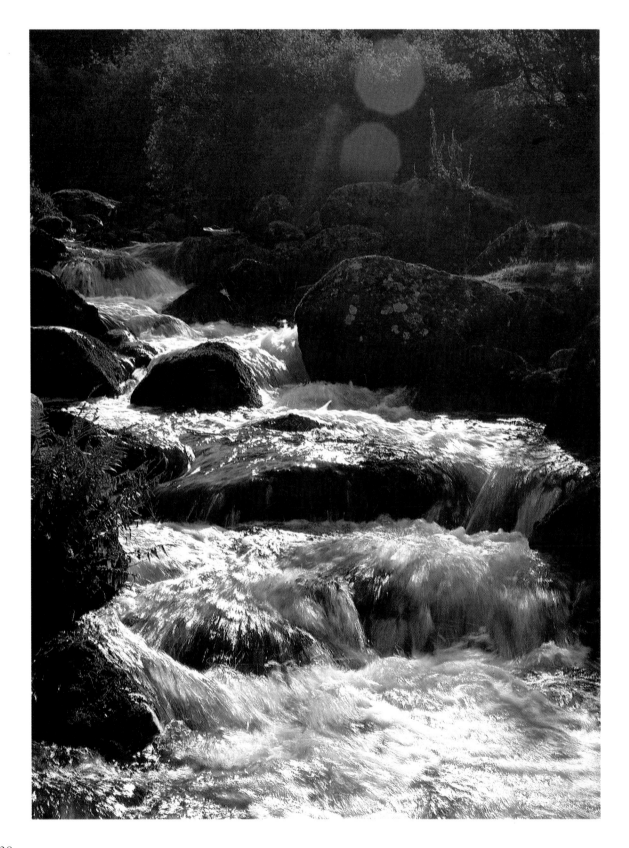

R away from the cliffs to visit the lower lake, and then walk along the shore to the next lake, which is very close by. This is the more impressive, though both are lovely. Walk from here over steep little heathery hummocks to the third lake in this corrie, the one nestling under the north-facing cliffs. This lake is backed by an evil-looking swamp that has been fenced in, presumably to keep sheep out.

Continue along the foot of the cliffs to Lough Coumfea, passing on the way the formidable pyramid of the mountain, also called Coumfea (2340 ft/713 m), soaring skyward and so much more impressive from below than on top. Walk the length of the lake on its R-hand side and continue north-west and north along a broad ridge towards fields on a bulge ahead. Before this bulge, cross a gate in a fence and then descend gradually towards the river R (it is the Nier again), keeping well above the thickly vegetated banks. Look out along here for the ruins of an old stone shelter 200 yards (180 m) from the near bank. From this shelter walk parallel to the river, following a path to a corner of wall. Take a track from here downhill (still parallel to the river), continuing straight ahead where it joins a farm road coming in from the R. Follow this round the hill L and back to the start.

The 'truly enormous flat boulder'

1   *Corries*

Corries, the deep hollows gouged out of the sides of the mountains, are a notable feature left from the Ice Age, and this is a good example of one. They were formed as the climate worsened at the onset of the cold. Snow gathered in north- and east-facing hollows sheltered from the prevailing winds and the sun. The snow solidified and accumulated over the years, eventually hollowing out a cliff-rimmed bed. Later still the solidified snow began to creep downhill, forming a glacier, to join other glaciers on the lower ground.

The hummocky ground below the corries on this route are moraines, rough unsorted rubble left behind by the snout of a glacier on its retreat at the end of an ice age.

Probably the finest corrie in Ireland, backed by cliffs 1400 ft (430 m) high, is at Coumshingaun, just to the east.

2   *The Dark Fisherman of Coumalocha*

Even though it is said to be haunted, fishermen are not afraid to spend the night at this lake. The spectre arises from the lake in the dead of night, takes the rod from fishermen who have caught no fish, catches trout for them and returns silently to the depths. This kindly ghost is called the Dark Fisherman of Coumalocha. If you are fishing, it is advisable not to rely entirely on him.

Opposite: *The River Nier*

2·4

THE LUGDUFFS

STARTING AND FINISHING
POINT
At the Visitor Centre at
Glendalough (124968). This is
reached by taking the R755/T61
to Laragh and then the
R756/L107 to Glendalough. The
Visitor Centre is on the L, and is
well signposted.
MAPS
The OS 1:50 000 Sheet 56 is
recommended. The OS Wicklow
District and the National Park
maps (at 1 inch to the mile and
1:25 000 respectively) are also
satisfactory, the latter depicting
the paths and tracks best of all.
LENGTH
8 miles (13 km)
ASCENT
1750 ft (540 m)

Glendalough, the village and valley, is a well-known monastic
site and beauty spot. On both sides of the valley's two lakes and
farther on to the west to bound a higher valley, Glenealo, run
lines of delectable hills, steepening in places towards Glenealo
into majestic cliffs. The southern line of these hills, a long ridge
of hummocky peaks, collectively called the Lugduffs, gives an
easy but spectacular stroll from Glendalough. This ridge is especially impressive on an eastern extension of the Lugduffs that
directly overlooks the Upper Lake at Glendalough. After the
Lugduffs, the walk descends into Glenealo, whose remote and
gentle charms contrast sharply with the tourist bustle of Glen-

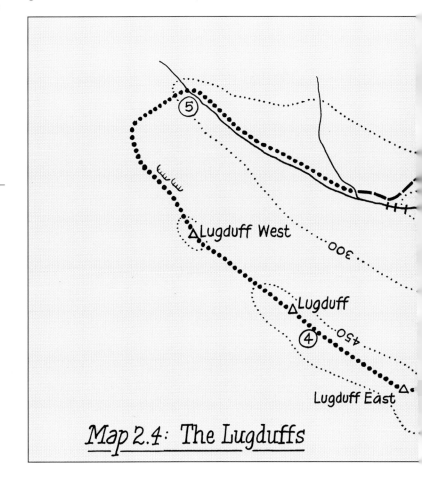

Map 2.4: The Lugduffs

dalough itself. The walk ends, as it began, along the scenic
wooded shores of the Upper and Lower Lakes.

Route Description (Map 2.4)

Turn L outside the Visitor Centre car-park, cross the village
bridge on a sharp L bend, and turn L off the road to walk through
the monastic site *(1)*. Cross the bridge beyond it and turn R onto
a pleasant tree-lined forest road *(2), (3)*, which passes to the L of
the Lower Lake. Directly ahead beyond the lake rises the
wooded Spink, towering over the Upper Lake — a fine initial
target to aim for. Take the second forest road steeply uphill,
crossing a bridge (signed 'Poll an Easa'), branching L off it to take
a path close to the cascade on the L.

At the top of the path rejoin the forest road and continue
upwards to a multiple junction of forest roads. Turn sharp R here
steeply uphill onto a forest road sign-posted 'Prezen Rock'.
Follow the road to the first bend L, leaving it here to climb a stile
on the R. Follow the path beyond diagonally uphill to the top of

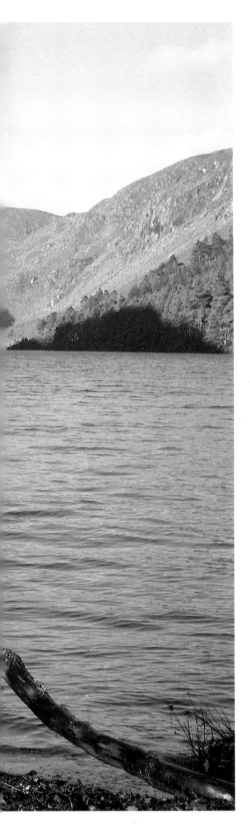

the Spink, where at the edge of the cliffs and with the magnificent trough sheltering the Upper Lake at your feet, you will doubtless conclude that the climb was well worth the effort.

Walk up the eroded path along the Spink so that the cliffs are on the R, continuing beyond the Upper Lake on what by here has become a track. Where this levels out (and here, in defiance of the maps, there are only scattered trees and clear-felled areas in the basin on the L) head directly towards the eastern end of the Lugduffs, picking up if fortunate an intermittent path.

Before starting along the Lugduffs, a word on navigation. The features on the Lugduffs do not lend themselves to determining your exact position, nor is it necessary that you should know it. However, if you do wish to know your position, the reservoir of the pumped storage station across the valley to the north provides a capital 'fix' (it has no other desirable attributes from a hillwalker's point of view).

Walk to Lugduff East and then to Lugduff itself over ground which, though soggy in places, allows good progress and offers magnificent views, south over the Lugnaquillia massif and north to Camaderry and beyond *(4)*. Lugduff (2154 ft/652 m), the highest of the family, is recognizable, apart from its cairn, by the great white quartzite boulders on the western side of its summit.

Walk onward to Lugduff West, after which a decisive drop into the col towards Conavalla marks the end of the Lugduffs. Turn R (north) in this col to reach the western end of the Glenealo Valley *(5)*. Cross the main stream in the valley and turn R to walk downstream on the L-hand bank along an intermittent path. At the start of the distinct drop into Glendalough the stream gathers force to drop in a series of waterfalls interspersed with tiny lakes that are partly hidden by thick vegetation. Around here the unpromising path graduates into an unexpectedly good track zigzagging down towards the Upper Lake, with steep ground clothed by occasional areas of trees on the R and boulders, scree and cliffs on the L.

Follow this track past the old mining ruins *(6)*, where it falters for a short distance, and then along the shore of the Upper Lake *(7)*. Just beyond the Upper Lake, cross a wooden bridge R, then follow the track beyond it parallel to the lake. Turn L at the fork and follow this forest road, the first of the day, back to the start.

The Upper Lake, Glendalough

Glenealo River

1   *The Monastic Site*

The monastic site at Glendalough is built around a monastery founded in the sixth century, which flourished as a place of learning and a focus for pilgrims until the twelfth century. The Round Tower dates from about the eleventh century and acted as a campanile and early-warning system against both foreign and native aggressors. Other buildings, mostly churches, are scattered along the valley to the east and west.

2   *Wicklow National Park*

Much of the area immediately south and west of here, covering 9400 acres (3800 hectares) and including nearly all the area covered by this walk, is in the Wicklow National Park. A separate area to the north covers 6900 acres (2800 hectares). It is hoped that eventually these two areas will be joined up and the total area greatly extended. There is an Information Centre for the park just before the climb to Poll an Easa.

3   *The Oakwoods*

The oakwoods here are probably a remnant of the great forests that once covered nearly all of Ireland. They were depleted in the Middle Ages to provide fuel and charcoal for mining.

4   *Bog Oak*

Watch out along the ridge of the Lugduffs for stumps of 'bog oak', partly exposed on the surface and in the peat hags (see p.14).

5   *The Large Mammals of Glenealo*

Herds of deer — sika, red and hybrids of the two — roam the entire area, grazing on the heath and bog vegetation. Of the three, the red deer is in danger of being overwhelmed by interbreeding. A band of feral goats also grazes in the Glenealo Valley and the adjacent mountains.

6   *Mining in Wicklow*

Mining for lead and copper was carried out in the nineteenth century and even for a short time in the 1920s. The zigzag track was originally a mining track. The metals occur along a metamorphic zone between the granite to the west and the older shales and slates to the east. Similar workings are evident in the glacial valleys north and south of here.

7   *The Disappearing Lakes*

The western shore of the Upper Lake has moved 130 yards (120 m) eastward in the last 80 years because of the wash-out from mining spoil, augmented by silt from the Glenealo River. In post-glacial times only one lake occupied the valley floor, but silt from the Poulanass River eventually split the lake in two.

SLIEVE BEARNAGH

STARTING AND FINISHING
POINT
At a car-park on the L of the
minor road (312314). From
Newcastle take the B180
(Hilltown road) forking L off it
onto the unclassified but labelled
Trassey Road 2.2 miles (3.5 km)
west of Bryansford. Drive onward
for 0.8 miles (1.3 km) to the car-
park.
MAPS
Northern Ireland OS 1:50 000
Sheet 29, or 1:25 000 Sheet
'Mourne Country'.
LENGTH
7 miles (11 km)
ASCENT
2850 ft (870 m)

Though the initial walk becomes a little tedious with long views precluded by an increasingly narrow slabby-sided glen, the first, sudden glimpse into the Silent Valley and across to the great arc of peaks around it makes the effort seem trivial. Slieve Bearnagh is the high point, literally and metaphorically, the sets of huge boulders on its summit adding a touch of the spectacular to an already impressive scene. The subsequent views, over the Meelmores and down by Fofanny Reservoir, are more gentle. The walk ends as it began on the Ulster Way. An easy introductory walk to the best of the Mournes.

ROUTE DESCRIPTION (Map 2.5)

Turn L out of the car-park *(1)*, pass the house on the L, and cross the gate L just beyond it to follow the Ulster Way *(2)*. Continue straight through another gate, thus leaving the Ulster Way, and walk up a wide track, ignoring R and L turns which lead to quarry workings *(3)*.

The Hare's Gap between Bearnagh and Slievenaglogh is the first target, and before it the track becomes not so much intermittent as indecisive, spreading heedlessly over a wide area, so that the gate at the gap in the Mourne Wall *(4)* ahead is a useful landmark. At the gap cross this gate *(5)*, so revealing the splendours of the Silent Valley and the high peaks of the Mournes beyond it.

Beyond the gate, turn immediately R to follow the Mourne Wall or, failing that, keep close to the steep slabs where the wall is not continuous. Climb to the two sets of gigantic piles of granite crowning the summit of Slieve Bearnagh (2425 ft/739 m), the first of which is called the North Tor and the other, a little way off, the Summit Tor. A good place to rest, explore among the boulders and admire the excellent views.

Descend steeply from Slieve Bearnagh towards Slieve Meelmore, the Mourne Wall still on the R, taking a short path that veers away from the Wall to avoid the Bearnagh Crags. At the col continue along the Mourne Wall (not the other wall, which veers L from it *(6)*) to reach the top of Slieve Meelmore (2310 ft/704 m), crowned by one of the occasional towers along the Wall *(7)*.

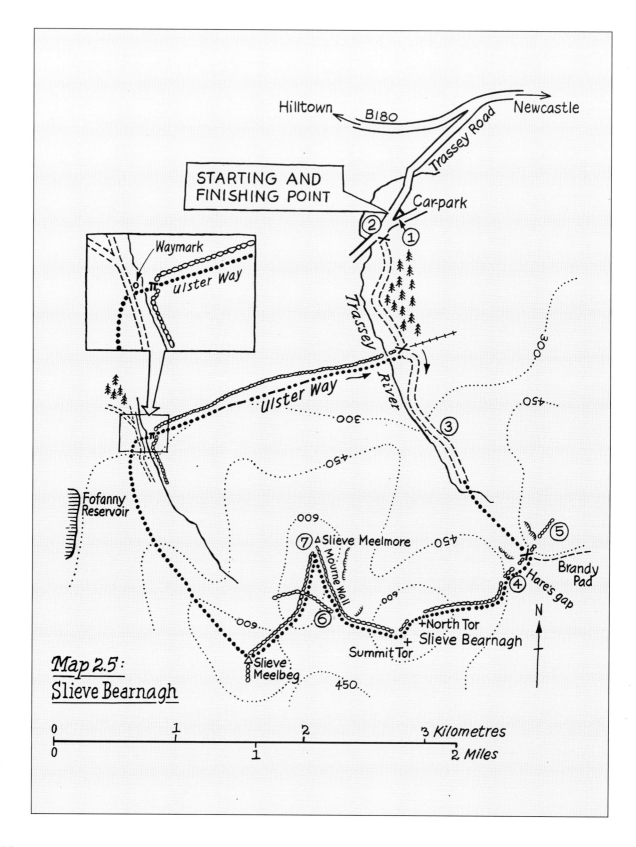

Hilltown   B180   Newcastle

Trassey Road

STARTING AND
FINISHING POINT

Car-park

②

①

Waymark

Ulster Way

Trassey River

Ulster Way

③

300

450

300

450

Fofanny
Reservoir

600

⑦ △Slieve Meelmore

Mourne Wall

450

⑤

Brandy
Pad

④   Hare's gap

N

600

North Tor
Slieve Bearnagh

600

⑥

Summit Tor

△Slieve
Meelbeg

450

Map 2.5:
Slieve Bearnagh

0   1   2   3 Kilometres

0   1   2 Miles

Hare's Gap (and the Mourne Wall)

From Meelmore follow the Wall down to the col and thence up to Slieve Meelbeg (2323 ft/708 m). Leave the Wall here to follow an intermittent and short-lived path down the north-west spur of Meelbeg with the Fofanny Reservoir prominent on the L and a wooded shore on the gentle slope behind it. Towards the bottom of the spur, veer R off it to meet an Ulster Way waymark, and follow the Way across a stream and over a stile.

Continue on the Ulster Way, with a wall on the L, all the way to the second gate of the day. Surprisingly, in an area of generally clear paths, this section of the Ulster Way is intermittent and the ground underfoot wet. At the gate, turn L and follow the Way back to the metalled road. Turn R for the car-park.

1 *The Cecil Newman Memorial*
   The simple stone memorial in the car-park commemorates Cecil Newman, a planner, who worked in the Northern Ireland Civil Service. He was among the first to recognize the necessity of planning for the mountain areas, particularly the Mournes.

2   *The Ulster Way*
    This was the first Long Distance Route in the island, and is still by far the longest. The route is about 440 miles (700 km) long and goes right round Northern Ireland, taking in a wide variety of terrain. Most of it is waymarked.

3   *The 'Plug and Feathers' Method*
    Look out along the way for wedge marks along the edges of granite stones. To split the quarried stones, rough holes were made in a line across the stone, and the plug (a small iron wedge) inserted between the feathers (two thin strips of steel).

4   *The Mourne Wall*
    This sturdily built wall, the most noteworthy granite wall in a land of such walls, is 22 miles (35 km) long and encloses the catchment area of the Silent Valley Reservoir. It was built as late as 1910–22 by local unemployed men using locally quarried stones, which were transported by handbarrows, no animals being used. The route of the Wall was until recently that of the Mourne Wall Walk, which attracted annually such huge numbers (several thousands) that it has wisely been abandoned.

5   *Diamond Rocks*
    A few hundred yards north-east of here are the Diamond Rocks where, if you have an abundance of patience, knowledge, skill and above all luck, you may chance upon almost worthless lodes of 'precious' crystalline stones such as topaz and quartz.

6   *The Stone Walls of Mourne*
    Drystone walls, of which the Mourne Wall is the most notable example, are a common feature of the Mournes. Local farmers neatly constructed them of undressed granite stones and boulders. They served as a boundary for sheep pastures.

7   *Meelmore and Meelbeg*
    'More' means big in Gaelic and 'beg' means small, but Meelmore is lower than Meelbeg by 13 ft (4 m). It is doubtful if the people who named the two mountains realized or would have cared about this seeming error. They probably named them on the basis of the apparent bulk as seen from where they lived.

The Tors on Slieve Bearnagh

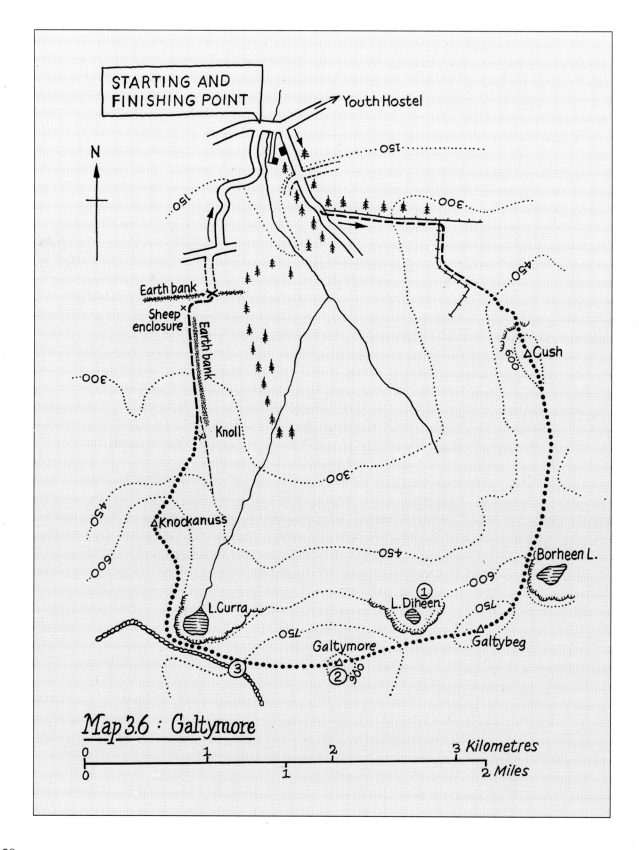

STARTING AND FINISHING POINT

Youth Hostel

N

Earth bank

Sheep enclosure

Earth bank

Knoll

△Knockanuss

△Cush

Borheen L.

L.Curra

① L.Diheen

Galtymore

Galtybeg

③

② Galtymore

Map 3.6 : Galtymore

0   1   2   3 Kilometres

0   1   2 Miles

3·6

GALTYMORE

STARTING AND FINISHING
POINT
At a turn-off on the south side of
the southernmost of the two Glen
of Aherlow roads (872281). From
Cahir take the N24 (Limerick
road) branching L off it after 6
miles (9.5 km) to follow signs for
Ballydavid Wood Youth Hostel.
Do not turn L up the side-road to
the Hostel; instead continue along
the Glen of Aherlow road. Pass
Condon's Pub on the R and across
a bridge 1.7 miles (2.7 km)
beyond it. Park on the waste
ground on the L just beyond the
bridge.
MAPS
The only maps available are the
OS half-inch to the mile series,
and both Sheets 18 and 22 are
needed for this walk. The
coverage of the Galtees is
inconveniently divided between
these two sheets; they have no
overlap, thus contributing to the
cartographic deficiencies of the
area.
LENGTH
8 miles (13 km)
ASCENT
3400 ft (1040 m)

The northern slopes of the Galtees rise abruptly as a series of
broad spurs from the rich agricultural dairy lands of south Tipperary. South of these spurs the otherwise smooth form of the
high east–west grassy ridge that forms the backbone of the range
is disrupted by a line of surprisingly deep and dramatic corries.
By ascending one spur and descending another the walk includes
the highest peak of the range and its one Munro, taking in on the
way the rims of three of the best corries in the range.

ROUTE DESCRIPTION (Map 3.6)

Cross back over the bridge and take the second turn R, a narrow,
metalled road. Keep on this where forest roads leave to R and L.
On emerging from forest on the L (it continues on the R), and
with Cush ahead displaying great blocks of rock on its otherwise
smooth R flank, cross a fence L to walk uphill along a rough path
with fence and forest close on the L. Cross one fence near the
crest of the hill and turn R to follow the path towards Cush.
Continue upwards where the fence swings R and climb steeply
over grass, and near the summit between conglomerate boulders, to Cush (2109 ft/643 m).
  Continue along the narrow ridge of Cush, and beyond it drop
to the boggy col towards Galtybeg (only at this point will the two
summits of Cush become evident). Climb over grass beyond the
col, fairly steeply at first and then more steeply, as far as Galtybeg, with the impressive corrie holding Borheen Lough on the
L. Galtybeg (2629 ft/801 m) commands excellent views, the
tiered cliffs of vertical rock in the next corrie, that of Lough
Diheen (1), each topped by a precarious ramp of grass, being
particularly impressive. Drop to the col and from there climb to
Galtymore (3018 ft/920 m), signalled by a cairn, the lower part
of an OS obelisk and a white cross and memorial plaque (2). The
view from here is exceptionally wide north and south, towards
the plains of Tipperary and beyond in one direction and towards
the Knockmealdowns in the other.
  Continue to the western end of the summit ridge to a large
cairn, dropping sharply beyond it to come within sight of a high
wall (3). Veer R to walk parallel to it, the corrie of Lough Curra

The Galtees across the Glen of Aherlow

on the R. Where the corrie rim veers R away from the wall follow the rim over the short climb to Knockanuss (2166 ft/660 m), descend along the spur north-west, veering R off it to pick up an earthbank near a small grassy knoll. Follow the earthbank down to enclosed land at a sheep enclosure. Turn R at another earthbank just beyond it and L through the first gate. Beyond it follow a track, which gradually improves to a metalled road as it gathers tributary lanes on its meandering route down-hill. Follow the metalled road to the main road and the starting point.

1   *Lough Diheen*

The corrie lake north-east of Galtymore attracted the rather gullible attention of the Halls, a husband and wife team who travelled around Ireland in the early 1840s. They uncritically re-told local stories that the lake was unfathomable, that if only a slight breeze blew across it the area round the lake became intensely cold, no matter how warm the day, and that in spite of its apparent narrowness a stone could not be thrown across it even when a champion in this simple sport

Cush and Galtybeg

hurled it. All this they, or rather the locals, attributed to a Pooka (ghost) which inhabited the lake. (A note for those interested in the inconsequential: the lake is about 80 yards (70 m) across, a considerable distance even for a champion stone-thrower.)

2   *The Plaque on Galtymore*
The plaque on the summit commemorates James Blake and Richard Hayward. James Blake was a local who, as the plaque states, died while trying to rescue a woman bather in Tangier. Richard Hayward was from far-off Belfast. He wrote many books and guides between 1922 and his death in 1964, mostly, but not exclusively, about his native Ulster. It is not clear why the two men are jointly remembered in this way.

3   *The Stone Wall*
This wall was built late in the nineteenth century to keep cattle away from the steep ground on the northern side of the hills, and also perhaps to define grazing boundaries. It is quite unusual for such a substantial wall to be built at this considerable height.

3·7

A TRAVERSE OF THE MOURNES

STARTING POINT

At a car-park (345219) on the mountain (that is, north) side of the C313 that runs from the Silent Valley east along the edge of the range. Take the A2 for 1 mile (1.6 km) north of Annalong, turning inland here, signposted 'Silent Valley 5', and drive straight ahead for 2.3 miles (3.7 km). Alternatively, take the C313 east from the gates of the Silent Valley Reservoir for 2.5 miles (4.0 km).

FINISHING POINTS

At Donard Park (375306), a major car-park at the south (that is mountain) side of Newcastle. The shorter route returns to the starting point.

MAPS

Northern Ireland 1:50 000 Sheet 29, or 1:25 000 Sheet 'Mourne Country'.

LENGTH

$6\frac{1}{2}$ miles (10.5 km) for the short route, $9\frac{1}{2}$ miles (15 km) for the long.

ASCENT

2100 ft (640 m) for the short route, 3950 ft (1200 m) for the long.

A traverse of the Mournes, south to north, is a moderately long but satisfying undertaking since it includes perhaps the finest peak, Slieve Binnian, and a selection of the best scenery in the range. This scenery is particularly good to the west — down into the Silent Valley and across to the great outcrops of Bearnagh. It must be admitted that the three peaks to be traversed north of Slieve Binnian are fairly undistinguished, and though they fall in impressive slabs to the east, they are a little dull on their western flanks. For this reason, a short route for returning to the start from Binnian is given. However, if you persevere with the longer route your efforts will be rewarded by good views to the town of Newcastle and northwards over lowlands and the coast beyond.

ROUTE DESCRIPTION (Map 3.7)

Take the track at the R of the car-park. Just over a $\frac{1}{2}$ mile (1 km) further up, pass through the far-right gate and continue along the track with a wall of gigantic boulders on the L (Mourne Wall). Keep close to the Wall where the track veers R, and climb steadily upwards all the way to the point where the Wall prudently, but only temporarily, discontinues at steep slabs almost at the top of Slieve Binnian. Cross the end of the Wall here and veer L under the slabs to reach the huge horizontal granite Summit Tor dominating the top of Slieve Binnian (2451 ft/747 m) (1).

From Binnian the route is quite simple. Take the path from the summit, first to the L of the huge boulders of the North Tor, and then continue downwards to the col facing Slievelamagan.

Short route Take a clear path R, which runs to the R of Blue Lough and thence to the main track of the Annalong Valley.

Long route Climb up the pathless — and relatively dull — slopes of Slievelamagan (2310 ft/704 m), drop to the col north of it and ascend Cove Mountain (2145 ft/655 m) keeping to the L of the direct route to avoid steep ground. From Cove, drop to a

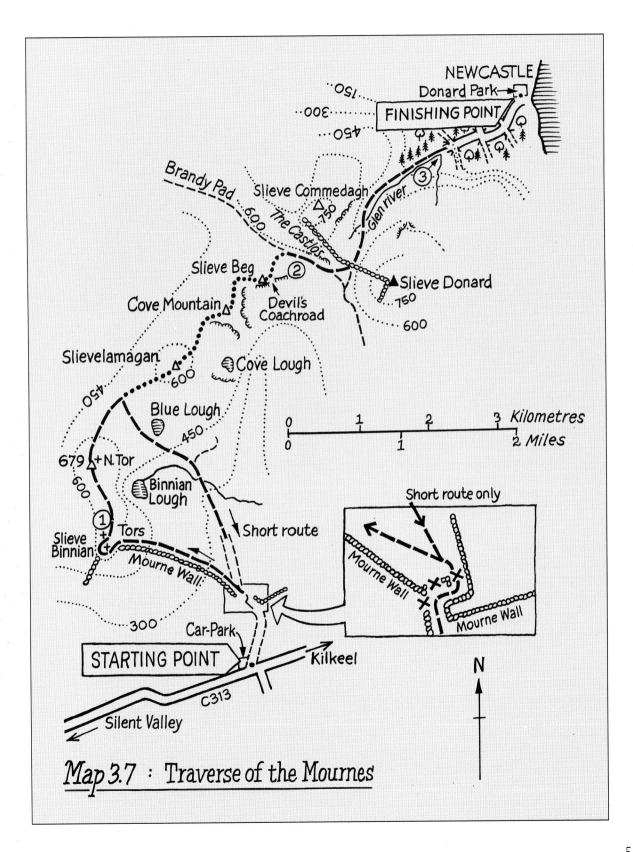

Map 3.7 : Traverse of the Mournes

Slieve Binnian from the south

sandy col towards Slieve Beg (about 1940 ft/590 m) and climb the peat-hagged slopes to the summit, a slightly unnecessary manoeuvre but worth it for the views it gives down cliffs pierced by a steep and narrow gully R, called the Devil's Coachroad. Drop a little to the col north and turn R onto the Brandy Pad *(2)*, the path which runs east–west across the southern slopes of Slieve Commedagh. Take the Pad under the cliffs of the Castles on the L, and beyond them leave it to climb L to the high pass between Commedagh and Slieve Donard. Cross the Mourne Wall at the pass and descend between cliffs towards the source of the River Glen, picking up a path that crosses the quickening stream R to L at its upper reaches *(3)*.

The aim now is to follow the stream down into Newcastle. Take the path downstream, crossing into forest at a stile. Cross over to the R bank at the second bridge down, and back to the L at the third, so keeping all the way to a path. Where the path joins a track further down on level ground turn R onto it, to keep close to the stream on the R. Keep on the track to the car-park just ahead.

1 *The Reservoirs of the Silent Valley*

The Silent Valley to the west cradles two major reservoirs. The larger, Silent Valley Reservoir dates from the 1930s and the smaller Ben Crom Reservoir to its north dates from 1957. Both reservoirs serve Belfast and surrounding areas.

2 *The Brandy Pad*

In the eighteenth and early nineteenth century the Brandy Pad was a favoured route of smugglers transporting wines and spirits, tobacco, tea, silk and (strangely) soap, all of which would have been landed from the Isle of Man onto deserted beaches. The goods were loaded onto ponies and taken under cover of darkness over the mountains west to Hilltown.

3 *The Ice House*

The igloo-like stone structure on the opposite bank, located just before forest is reached, is an 'ice-house', which once functioned as a primitive refrigerator. Since the owners of the ice-house lived down in Newcastle, a certain amount of forethought would have been needed in deciding what was required from it.

Ben Crom Reservoir and Slieve Bearnagh (centre)

LUGNAQUILLIA AND THE GLEN OF IMAAL

In the Glen of Imaal at a junction on a side-road (982948). Take the N81 to the junction on the east (L from Dublin) for Donard and go straight through the village, watching out for the slightly offset crossroads here. Pass the Youth Hostel and drive straight ahead for another 1.6 miles (2.6 km) to a side road R and a cryptic and oddly worded Army injunction on a signboard on the L reading 'WALKING ROUTE FOLLOW'. Park carefully on the grass around here. (A note for the faint-hearted: this starting point facilitates an escape route from the pass between Imaal and Glenmalure.)

MAPS

The OS 1:50 000 Sheet 56 map is recommended. The Wicklow District one-inch to the mile map, though not quite as useful, is adequate.

LENGTH

15½ miles (25 km)

ASCENT

3400 ft (1050 m)

Lugnaquillia at 3039 ft (925 m) is the highest mountain in Ireland outside Kerry, the qualification admittedly being extremely significant. It stands at the centre of a series of spurs reaching starfish-like in all directions and so allows a good variety of routes up one spur, down another. Though the summit is an unimpressive grassy plateau, the views it provides are excellent, particularly to the north. The high-level gradual descent in this direction, included in this route, extends and modifies these views and turns a simple mountain climb into an impressive circuit.

ROUTE DESCRIPTION (Map 4.8)

Facing away from the Army board, take the side-road south through an area of scattered trees past the memorial on the L *(1)*, over a bridge spanning the Little Slaney River and up to the hamlet of Seskin. Turn L here along a rough road which ends at a T-junction. Continue straight ahead through a gate onto a track marked by an occasional Army waymark. Walk steadily upwards on this track, which further on narrows to a path to reach the top of Camarahill (1567 ft/480 m), an undistinguished outlier of Lugnaquillia.

Drop slightly beyond Camarahill, after which continue the steady climb, which steepens onto a rocky shoulder as the summit plateau of Lugnaquillia nears. Walk across the short grass to reach the huge cairn marking the summit at 3039 ft (925 m). The mountain indicator here points to an impressive array of peaks, including some in Wales. To obtain the widest panorama it is necessary to walk a little way from the cairn, an effort far outweighed by the consequent dramatic, broad views.

The descent from Lugnaquillia is an easy and scenic one. Walk north-east and then north-west, with the shoulder of Cannow to the L, so keeping to the high grassy ground. Along this initial stretch pick up a good path which continues all the way down to the boggy ground facing Camenabologue. On this gradual

SAFETY NOTE

The area enclosed by this route is a military artillery range. Do not diverge to the L of the route. If firing is taking place, the whole area (including this route) will be out of bounds. Though firing is infrequent it is imperative that you check with the Army authorities before setting out: Tel: 045–54626 or 045–54653.

descent watch out for the rounded hills to the R of the path, whose high ground may mislead the unwary into wandering east. On a more cheerful note, look out also for the great whale-back peak of Tonelagee prominent ahead, and the tiny Art's Lough across a valley to the R of the route *(2)*.

From the low point climb Camenabologue (2495 ft/758 m) through a rocky area, and northwards beyond it descend through peat hags to the indistinct pass between the Glen of Imaal and Glenmalure *(3)*, *(4)*, a pass marked by Army signposts. Here you may wish to return directly to the starting point. If so, take the clear path directly west following a line of Army waymarks down through open moorland, along an untidy forest road and through an area of pleasant deciduous trees to the start.

Map 4.8: Lugnaquillia and the Glen of Imaal

For the full route continue north at the pass to the cairn on Table Mountain (2302 ft/702 m), a mountain which lives up to its unflattering name all too well. Continue north-west from Table across a broad, windswept expanse of bogland, aiming for the long spur running west on the northern side of the Glen of Imaal. Along the initial stretch from Table, a wide but intermittent ditch develops, a useful aid in navigating all the way to Lobawn.

Once on the spur the route is generally downwards, the two rises being an unusually green unnamed hill east of Kavanagh's Gap and the rise to Lobawn itself (2097 ft/636 m), a grassy peak crowned by a WD (War Department) pillar. From Lobawn head on a dog-leg south and then west to Sugarloaf (1817 ft/554 m), following a clear path on the westward stretch. The descent from Sugarloaf is steep and gorse-impeded. Aim a little north of west and at forest turn L downhill to a point where the boundary fence is supplemented by horizontal wooden poles. Beyond these, two lines of fencing run directly into the forest (it is important to find this point). Cross the boundary fence and walk between the two lines of fencing on a narrow path, and beyond it keep close to the fence on the L. Turn L with this fence to a grassy track which can be reached using a stile.

Turn L onto the track and follow it on the level, and later downhill, first through deciduous and then through coniferous trees to a metalled road. Turn L here for a direct walk to the starting point *(5)*.

1   The Memorial in the Glen
The memorial here honours four officers and 12 other ranks of the Irish Army who were killed at Leitrim Mountain near here in 1941. Twenty others were injured, 12 of them seriously. The accident occurred when a fuse failed during a demonstration of the operation of an anti-tank mine. Curiously, the report of this major accident in the local newspaper merited as much space as cake-making competitions in nearby villages.

In 1979 three children were killed and nine injured in a shell explosion in this area while they were throwing 'scrap metal' around. Since then, security around the range has been greatly tightened.

Looking across the top of Glenmalure

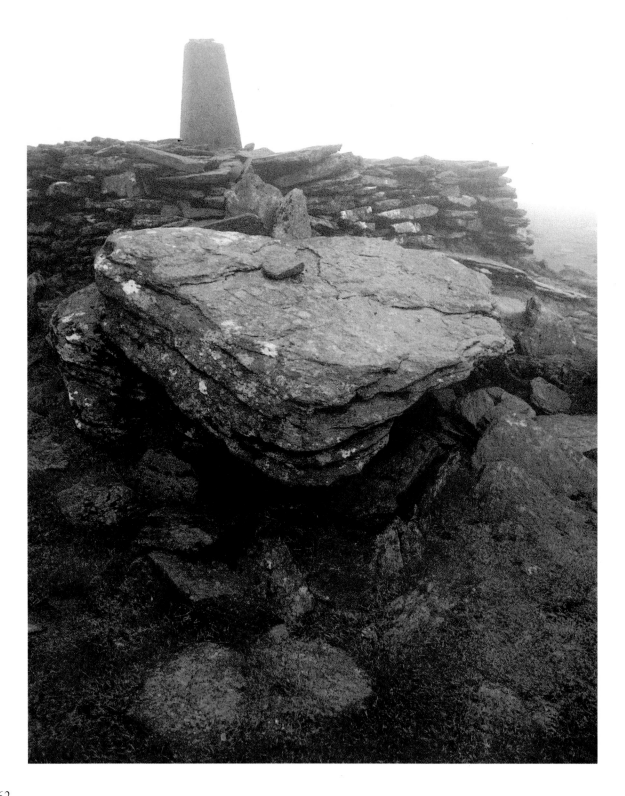

The Glen of Imaal Artillery Range has been used by both the British Army in its time, and later by the Irish Army. On the walk you will see several 'WD' pillars, indicating the boundary of War Department territory.

2   *River Basin and Glacial Valley*

The contrast here between the broad, shallow river basin to the west (Imaal) and the deep, narrow glacial valley to the east (Glenmalure) is very striking. In this range as elsewhere glaciers tended to form on the north and east of the mountains, where shelter from the prevailing westerlies and the sun allowed snow to accumulate.

3   *The Pass between Glenmalure and Imaal*

Until the last century, coach and horse could use the track between the two glens and there was frequent communication between them. The track is now almost non-existent near the top of the pass to the east.

4   *Three Lakes*

The two lakes seen ahead are called 'Three Lakes'. If there ever was a third lake it has long since dried up.

5   *Irish Elk in Ballinclea Bog*

The skull and much of the antlers of an Irish elk (*Megacerous hibernicus*) were dug out of the bog near here during drainage operations in 1983. The elk, which lived 7000–10 000 years ago, was about the size of a horse, with antlers 12 ft (3.7 m) across.

Summit of Lugnaquillia

Introduction

This region comprises the large, sprawling county of Donegal and the area to its south in Sligo, which is geographically close but geologically far distant from it. Backing a rugged indented northern coast, the core of the region consists of the great ranges of hills, much of them over 2000 ft (610 m), stretching in parallel lines south-west to north-east; Errigal to Muckish, and the Derryveagh and Glendowan Mountains. Each range is bare and unforested and each separated from its neighbours by lowland bog or lake. The clear-cut orientation of these hills reminds one of the Scottish Highlands and no wonder, since they belong to the same mountain-building epoch. Indeed, not only the hills echo Scotland; the people of Donegal have more than a touch of the Scot about them in accent and in their forthright manner, accentuated by the seasonal migration to Scotland that has long been a tradition here.

South of this core area, in a wide band across the centre of Donegal, are lower and less rugged mountains degenerating in more than a few places into windswept moorland. In the south-west of Donegal is a great area of mountain bulging westward which includes the massive cliffs of Slieve League and, fronting Donegal Bay, a tangle of muted mountains and high ground which has just a trace still of the south-west to north-east trend of north Donegal. A route along the sea-cliffs at Slieve League has been omitted. Of course the cliffs are spectacular but it is essentially an unchanging spectacle with a dull landward side. In addition, access is difficult.

The scarplands and tiny but rugged hills of Sligo (and Leitrim) across Donegal Bay are quite different to any part of Donegal, or to anywhere else in Ireland for that matter. This is a gentle and less wild area with strong literary and poetic associations, though the attractions for the walker are far from minor.

Seven walks in this area have been included. One representative sample from the Sligo area was essential, and the plateau of Ben Bulben, the name widely associated in both poetic and mountaineering terms with the whole area, gives as good a walk as any and better than most. The Bluestacks, the highest group in the south of Donegal at just over 2000 ft (610 m) was perhaps an odd choice, given their gently moulded summits and semi-aqueous

Lough Eske from the Blue Stacks

fringes. Nevertheless, it is an area whose subtle pleasures are reserved for those who are prepared to persevere.

The remaining five routes encompass the great heartland of north Donegal. The lake and Castle of Glenveagh, the focal point of a National Park, provides a rare opportunity for a short walk combined with a visit to an elegant house and gardens. Two routes, the circuit of the Poisoned Glen and the climb to Slieve Snaght, are both in the lofty Derryveagh Mountains. The former route approaches the range from the north, so taking in the scarred cliffs almost surrounding the wild, strangely-named defile. The latter's goal is the great dome-shaped peak, at 2240 ft (683 m) the highest in the range. The approach is from the south where the frowning cliffs of the Bingorms confront the low and boggy shores of Lough Barra.

Errigal and Muckish are the two best-known mountains in Donegal. And deservedly so, because they are two fine peaks. Taken separately they do not form good, looped walks, but together they give a tough but highly attractive route. Lastly, on the rugged, indented coastline facing north against the Atlantic is a walk on Horn Head peninsula, one of several impressive promontories in the region.

1·9

GLENVEAGH

STARTING AND FINISHING
POINT
At Glenveagh Castle (021209) in
Glenveagh National Park. The
entrance to the National Park is
on the R251/L82 and is well
signposted. A bus takes visitors
from the Visitor Centre near the
entrance as far as the Castle —
cars are not allowed. There is a
small charge for this service. The
bus does not operate in winter.
MAP
The Park authorities issue an
adequate one inch to the mile
map at the entrance. If not
available Northern Ireland OS
Sheet 1 or Republic of Ireland OS
Sheet 1 (both half-inch to the
mile) suffices.
LENGTH
6 miles (9.5 km) for the short
route; 7 miles (10.5 km) for the
long.
ASCENT
400 ft (120 m) for the short;
1100 ft (340 m) for the long.
ACCESS
Walking off paths may be
restricted in winter to facilitate
deer culling. For details telephone
074–37090.

Glenveagh Castle, the focal point of Glenveagh National Park, and the starting point of this walk, is an oasis of sophisticated civilization in a desert of natural wildness. The Castle and its gardens stand on the shores of Lough Veagh, which in turn occupies a long, straight, beautiful valley, almost entirely unwooded except for a plague of rhododendrons on the hillside. The whole atmosphere of the area is as much Scottish as Irish, a feeling enhanced by the red deer that roam the hillsides. Both the routes given explore the narrow main valley and even narrower side valley, in which mixed woodland softens the otherwise bleak valley floor. Both give views of the spectacular three-tiered Astelleen waterfall. The long route, in addition, samples the high moorland, so giving long views of neighbouring peaks for comparatively little effort.

ROUTE DESCRIPTION (Map 1.9)

Short route From behind the Castle *(1)* walk south-west on a clear track to the end of Lough Veagh; that is, keep it on the R *(2), (3)*. Just beyond it, past a small cottage tucked into the bank on the R, turn back L steeply uphill onto a side track not shown on the map issued by the Park authority. Keep on this to walk through a mixed wood and later into a narrow, open valley. Turn back where the track loses itself in rough wet country and retrace your steps to the Castle.

Long route Walk along the lake as described above, but continue straight ahead on the main track where the side track branches L. Pass to the R of the stalking cottage. Where the track swings L and then R and immediately passes a copse of beeches on the L, the first point where rhododendrons do not block the upper slopes, ascend L up a steep, wet, pathless hillside. At the top, between the two muted peaks of Farscollop ('Scollops' on the Park authority's map), cross the narrow, flat saddle and descend on the other side into a very wet side valley of the main valley.

Turn L and walk along an initially treeless, pathless stretch which further on gives way to a mixed wood in a narrow steep-sided valley. Follow the track which gradually emerges, keeping to it as far as the main track. Turn R onto this for the Castle.

Map 1.9 : Glenveagh

1   *Glenveagh National Park*
The Park covers 24,600 acres (10,000 ha) and includes a long
line of mountains running north-east from Slieve Snaght as
well as lower ground to the south-east of Lough Veagh. Part
of Errigal is a detached segment. The Interpretative Centre

Lough Veagh

near the entrance car-park gives a fine overview of all aspects of the Park, including its geology and fauna and flora.

The Castle, a castellated four-storey mansion made from rough-hewn granite, was built about 1870 and it and its extensive gardens were donated to the state by its American owner in 1981. Both Castle and gardens are open to the public. It is a tribute to the attentive work of the planners and gardeners that a variety of exotic plants from as far away as Chile, Madeira and Tasmania thrive here in such unpromising and unlikely surroundings, sheltered by pines and rhododendrons. Sculptures and other formal features counterbalance the otherwise informal layout of the gardens.

2 *Derrybeg Bog*
The small bog at the south-west end of Lough Veagh is slightly dome-shaped like a raised bog, but its vegetation is more akin to that in a lowland blanket bog; that is, it is dominated by grass and sedge, and not shrub and moss as in the raised bogs. This bog has been classified as being of national importance.

3 *The Glenveagh Evictions*
Glenveagh was the scene of a notorious series of evictions in 1861. The landlord, John George Adair, evicted all 254 of his tenants in that year after a steward was murdered and sheep stolen. People horrified by these evictions paid the passage of the former tenants to Australia, where they founded a settlement named after their far-off native place.

Opposite: *A stream in Glenveagh*

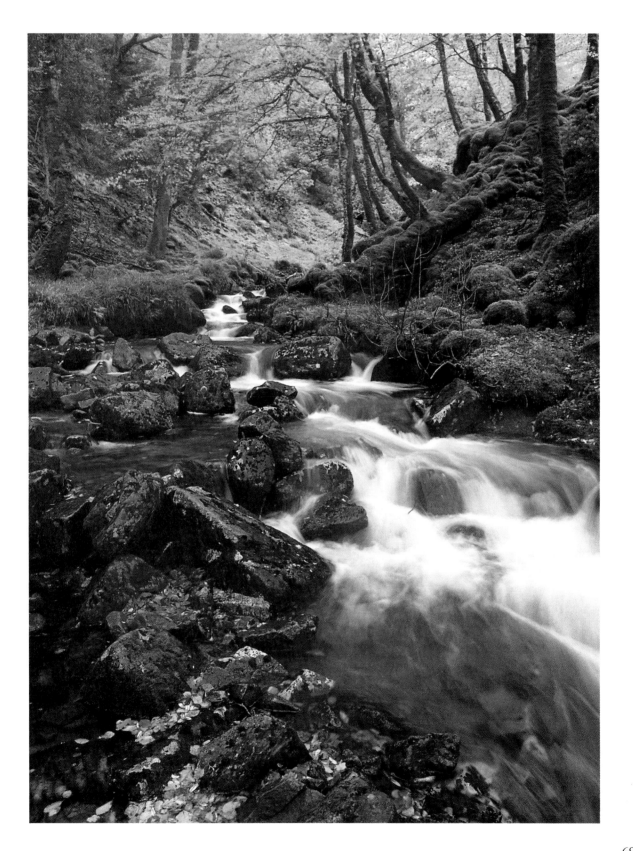

2·10

SLIEVE SNAGHT

STARTING AND FINISHING POINT

Just north of Lough Barra on the R254 (Doocharry to Church Hill road) (938134). Park near the farmhouse that has a thick shelter belt of trees, the only one for miles, on both sides of the road.

MAPS

Northern Ireland OS Sheet 1 or Republic of Ireland Sheet 1 (both half-inch to the mile). The entire route is also shown on the Glenveagh National Park one-inch to the mile map and this is better than either of the half-inch ones.

LENGTH

5 miles (8 km)

ASCENT

2000 ft (610 m)

Slieve Snaght is a fine peak, a great granite dome whose rocky flanks glisten in the fleeting sunlight which frequently follows rain. At 2240 ft (683 m) it is the highest of the Derryveagh Mountains, a range which exhibits to perfection the north-east to south-west orientation of the mountains of north Donegal. The peak can be approached from the north at Dunlewy, a route which entails a long walk-in, or from the south by a shorter approach, the one chosen here. A minor road runs through countryside of desolate splendour giving a long but memorable drive to the start. The route penetrates the south-west end of the great barrier of the Bingorms, a fine line of cliffs, crags and gullies. After climbing Slieve Snaght and exploring the tangled terrain of dyke and lakelet to its north-east, the route descends gently around this barrier's northern side.

ROUTE DESCRIPTION (Map 2.10)

From the farmhouse, walk south-west (that is, with high ground on the R) for 350 yards (300 m) along the road to a bridge, cross it and turn immediately R onto a rough, intermittent path along a stream, the Sruhanerolee River *(1)*. Follow it into the wet upper basin, keeping to slightly higher ground L to avoid the soggiest terrain. Climb up beside the high waterfall at the end of the basin (not the waterfall on the R), keeping to the shelving slabs if you have sufficient friction and nerve.

At the top of the waterfall, cross the stream to head north-east to Slieve Snaght (there is no need to continue to the top of the col), a stiff ascent with several crags to surmount or evade and at least one intermediate cairn and several false summits to cause disappointment. Slieve Snaght, crowned by a fine cairn, gives excellent views in all directions, those north and north-east to Errigal and the Aghlas being particularly good.

From Slieve Snaght continue in approximately the same direction north-east to the side of Lough Slievesnaght, a lake tucked into a bleak but highly scenic rocky mountainside. From its northern end take the conspicuous grassy ramp towards the southern Rocky Cap Mountain, so avoiding long and steep crags to the L.

Map 2.10 : Slieve Snaght

After the initial climb towards Rocky Cap there is a curious area of tiny dykes cradling lakelets *(2)*. Some sections of the walls of the dykes are in the form of rough, square granite blocks, with one rock in particular protruding precariously over a dizzying void. Walk to the small cairn on the southern Rocky Cap (about 1700 ft/520 m) and continue towards, but not to, the northern top. At a lake with crags falling directly into its near side (Lough Slievesnaghtbeg), a larger one than those so far encountered around this peak, turn R (i.e., south-east) thus heading along a narrow valley.

Continue down into a wide, wet basin following the Sruhan-cronahurney River, the major stream. Veer R from the stream as you descend, to emerge onto the road at a bridge initially hidden by cliffs R, and turn R for the starting point.

1   *Lough Barra Bog*
South-west of Lough Barra and partly visible on the ascent is Lough Barra Bog, a lowland blanket bog with numerous pools and lakelets that make it hazardous to explore. The river that flows through it is a habitat for Greenland white-fronted geese, golden plover and merlins.

The Sruhanerolee River

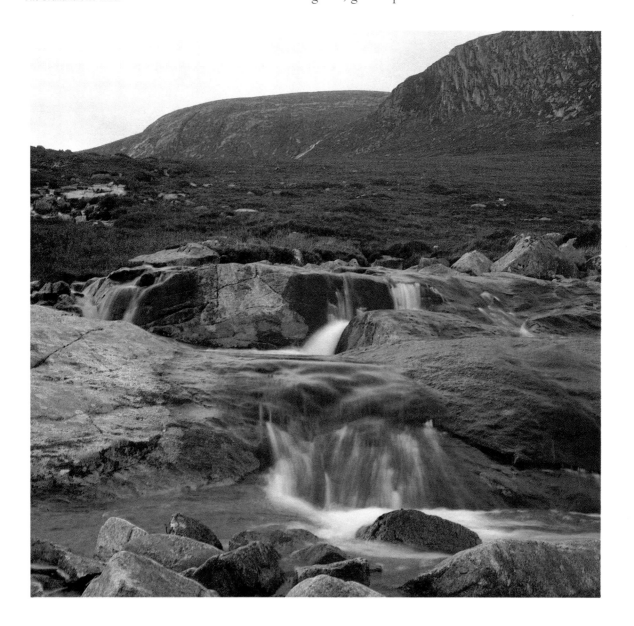

2   *The Dykes*

The narrow, straight and often long trenches which are crossed on this and Route 13 mark the lines of igneous dykes. During a geologically recent volcanic era hot magma was thrust vertically up from below the earth's crust to cleave the pre-existing rock, here granite. The upthrust rock, also granite, proved to be less durable than the metamorphozed pre-existing rock and has been worn down quicker by erosion, thus leaving the present-day trenches.

These dykes are well displayed on an aerial photograph at the Visitor Centre at Derryveagh National Park.

Peat cuttings

2·11

HORN HEAD

STARTING AND FINISHING POINT

At a side turn on Horn Head peninsula (017382). Take the signposted road off the N56 at Dunfanaghy, drive across Horn Head bridge and park at the side-road on L, 0.7 miles (1.1 km) further on.

MAPS

Northern Ireland OS Sheet 1 or Republic of Ireland OS Sheet 1 (both half-inch to the mile) are adequate.

LENGTH

$7\frac{1}{2}$ miles (12 km)

ASCENT

800 ft (240 m)

SAFETY NOTE

The initial part of the route is difficult to follow in summer when the bracken is high. In addition, the pleasant walk along the beach at the start is severely restricted when the tide is in. If this is the case take the road, not the·rough country behind the beach, to avoid an impassable stretch of vegetation.

On a rugged coastline dominated by cliff-bound headlands and long, surf-fringed inlets, Horn Head peninsula is probably the most spectacular. Bounded on the east by Sheep Haven and the headland of Rosguill, and on the west by a long sweep of desolate shoreline reaching to Bloody Foreland, it offers excellent long views of sea-cliff and coastal scenery backed on the landward side by the high peaks of Muckish and its western neighbours.

The walk, one of several that can be easily devised on the peninsula, is along the more rugged eastern side. It starts quietly enough at sea-level. Gradually the tempo quickens along a low ragged coastline and over a shaggy headland until finally one faces the towering quartzite cliffs of Horn Head itself rising sheer 626 ft (191 m) from the surging ocean. The return is more placid; an easy stroll by road through the rough moorland at the centre of the peninsula.

ROUTE DESCRIPTION (Map 2.11)

Continue along the road that you arrive on *(1)* and descend to the beach where the road rises and continues straight ahead. Walk along the beach noting thick vegetation centred on a small stream which issues onto the beach *(2)*. Beyond it, climb the low, grassy slope and continue parallel to the shore, keeping it on the R.

A word about the long stretch from here to Horn Head. There are numerous paths wending here and there, each offering some help to the walker but none giving a definitive route. In the wild, rough and rising ground to the Head you must navigate without a sure path, a not over-difficult task given that the sea is always to be kept on the R and that, in case of difficulty, there is generally a road not too far off on the L.

Follow a wall which runs parallel to the shore to an inlet on the R, and then continue past an amphitheatre sheltering an array of plants, which thrive in the comparatively calm ecosystem. Beyond this are a few curious, flat-topped islands and peninsulas. At the last of these, Duncap Isle, the coast swings from north to west to reveal Traglisk Point with the ruined Signal Tower on its shoulder. After this turn, climb along the shoulder of Croaghna-maddy and beyond it continue along what is now a high cliff *(3)*

74

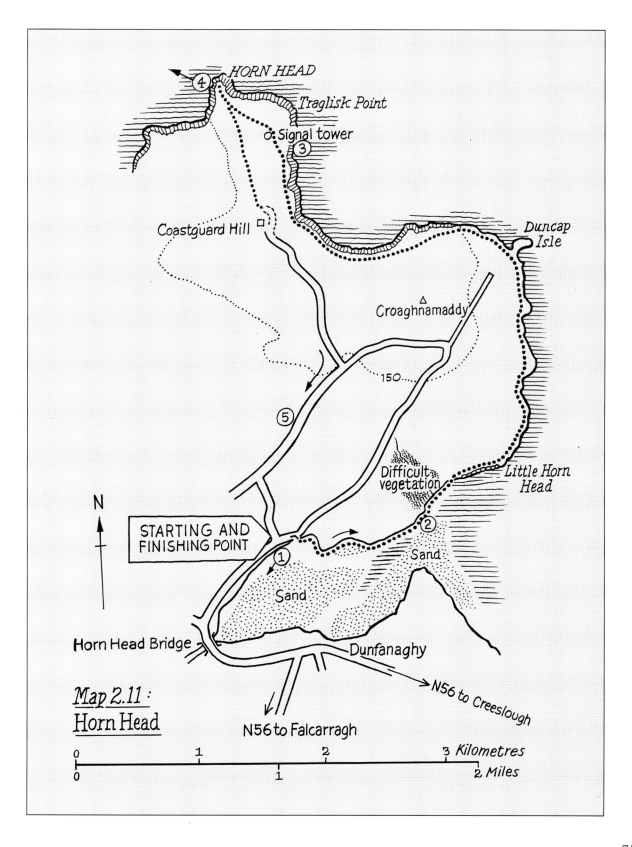

HORN HEAD

④

Traglisk Point

♂ Signal tower
③

Coastguard Hill

Duncap Isle

△
Croaghnamaddy

150

⑤

Difficult
vegetation

Little Horn
Head

N

STARTING AND
FINISHING POINT

②

Sand

①

Sand

Horn Head Bridge

Dunfanaghy

N56 to Creeslough

Map 2.11 :
Horn Head

N56 to Falcarragh

0   1   2   3 *Kilometres*
0   1   2 *Miles*

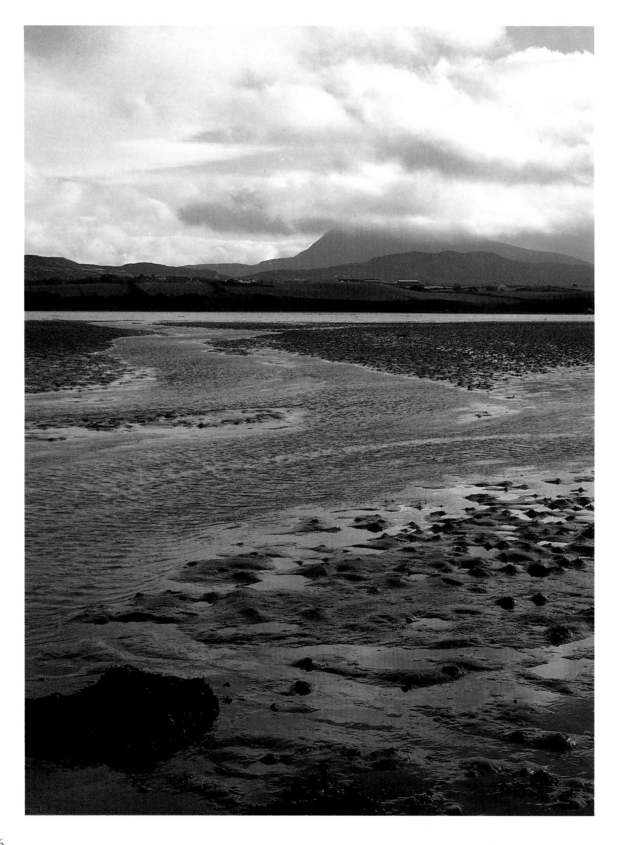

past the Signal Tower. From here the two projecting peaks of Horn Head itself are a short distance away over short grass *(4)*.

To return, retrace your outward route keeping more to the R of the Signal Tower, over rough, boggy ground, and ascend towards (not to) the blockhouse on Coastguard Hill. Take the track which curls round the near side of the hill and walk the short stretch to a metalled road. Continue straight ahead where a road comes in on the L (this is the Horn Head scenic drive and is not shown on the maps) *(5)*. Turn L at the junction marked 'Horn Head 4 km' (the previous sign which measured the distance at 3 km is 1 mile/1.6 km away) and follow it downhill to the starting point.

The start of the walk

1 *The New Lake*
   Horn Head peninsula was an island until as late as the eighteenth century, when the sand dunes to the south-west of the present peninsula developed. The area south of Horn Head bridge was a tidal estuary until the twentieth century, when it was sealed by westward-blowing sand encouraged by over-cutting of the marram sand at Tramore Strand. The OS maps still show the estuary, and not the freshwater New Lake which formed as a result.

2 *A Treacherous Coast*
   Note the ribs of wrecked ships half-buried in the sand around here.

3 *The Seabirds of Horn Head*
   The vertical or near-vertical quartzite cliffs here are a favourite nesting area for a variety of birds, including kitti-wakes, guillemots, razorbills and puffins. Other birds which breed around here include the peregrine falcon, raven, rock pipit and chough.

4 *Tory Island*
   Tory Island, one of the most remote of the inhabited islands off the Irish coast, is visible from the Head on clear days, 9 miles (15 km) away to the west, its almost entirely cliff-bound southern side making it unmistakable. The islanders, who number about 200, are Gaelic-speaking. The East Town, on the near side from Horn Head, is a *clachan* (see p. 15) reputedly the most authentic in Ireland.

5 *Fuchsia*
   The shrub fuchsia grows in unusual profusion along the hedgerows here, which are as thick and abundant as the fields they enclose are narrow and barren. Its red or purple bell-like flowers last from July all the way through to October.

Opposite: *Muckish from Horn Head*

BEN BULBIN

On a minor road south of the Ben Bulbin plateau (714424). From Sligo take the N15, turn R at the church in Rathcormack (signposted 'Glencar $4\frac{1}{2}$'). Turn R at the T-junction after 1 mile (1.6 km) and park 1.4 miles (2.2 km) further on near the prominent guesthouse on the L.

FINISHING POINT
On the same minor road as above at a crossroads at 689436. From the starting point, drive back along the road for 1.9 miles (3.0 km), to a slightly offset crossroads with a metalled road R and farm road L.

MAPS
Northern Ireland OS Sheet 3 or Republic of Ireland OS Sheet 7 (both half-inch to the mile). (OS 1:50 000 Sheet 16 is scheduled for end 1991.)

LENGTH
$6\frac{1}{2}$ miles (10.5 km)

ASCENT
1700 ft (520 m)

SAFETY NOTE
The Ben Bulbin plateau is featureless, so it is difficult to fix one's position in bad visibility. It is also mostly surrounded by cliffs and steep ground. Fortunately, *most* of the cliffs are immediately evident because they are sheer and abrupt. Most also drop directly from the top of the

Ben Bulbin, an area immortalized by W. B. Yeats, is one of a group of plateaus to the east of Sligo town. From the lowlands the slopes below each plateau appear as a steeply rising grassy bank topped by a fearsome layer of dark limestone, so fearsome and forbidding that it is something of an anticlimax to discover that the plateau itself is flat moorland. It is as if the land that the maps optimistically labelled 'here be dragons' turn out to be solely the abode of slugs. However, the walk reaches the Ben Bulbin plateau by traversing one of the great gullies that cleave it open, on the way giving excellent views over scenic Glencar. Once there, one can admire a wide sweep of coast and the neighbouring section of the plateau's rim, though not the out-of-sight section at one's feet. The return is by an easy grassy slope and pleasant country roads.

ROUTE DESCRIPTION (Map 2.12)

Go through the gate on the L of the guesthouse as one faces it and up the lane. Cross another gate further up and continue on to a derelict house. Here the lane ends so continue upwards across two rough fields, climb the steep but short rise beyond them and carefully cross the wall on the L into open country.

The good track into King's Gully is the next objective. With a plentitude of false trails hereabouts, perhaps the best plan is to head diagonally upwards *(1)* towards the gully, avoiding numerous rocks that have fallen from the cliffs above (especially if they are still moving). Once on the track, take it into the R side of the gully *(2)* and where it swings sharply back R continue straight ahead on a path, which peters out at about the same point as the gully softens to a steep but narrow valley.

Cross this valley onto the Ben Bulbin plateau *(3)*, a region of soft boggy ground and occasional peat hags, and head north-west (a compass bearing is advisable) to climb a rounded hill. Beyond it descend slightly to a narrow neck of high ground, keeping to the R of the promontory to admire the long stretch of coast round Donegal Bay.

Keep the cliffs on the R to Ben Bulbin (1722 ft/525 m). This has an OS obelisk which, if you didn't know that it was on a lofty plateau, so that the walker is unlikely to encounter cliffs low down on the descent, a disheartening experience. Nonetheless, care should be taken to avoid steep ground when coming off the plateau in poor visibility.

site, would appear to be inexplicably located in a flat boggy field. From Ben Bulbin continue round the plateau, sheer cliffs still on the R. Where they relent, drop gradually over rough ground to the upper end of a fence by an infant stream in a hint of a valley (in bad weather head to the R of the direct route, to make sure that you hit the fence). Follow the fence directly downhill on its far side to a grove of hawthorn and below it cross a gate on the R. Take the track beyond past a L turn (ignore it), and at a metalled road just ahead turn L (this may be better described as continuing

Map 2.12 : Ben Bulbin

The prow of Ben Bulbin

straight ahead). Take the first side-turn L and follow it parallel to the rim of the plateau, and then directly away from it. The end of the walk is at the minor road (see STARTING POINT) which, given the really minor roads you have just walked, will now probably appear quite major.

1   *Drumcliff Church*
Sligo and the surrounding area was beloved of Ireland's national poet, W. B. Yeats, and it is in the little churchyard at Drumcliff 'under bare Ben Bulben's head' that he is buried (the spelling of 'Ben Bulbin' varies). The church tower is easily visible on this ascent at the north-east corner of Drumcliff Bay. Many of Yeats's most famous poems describe and indeed immortalize this area.

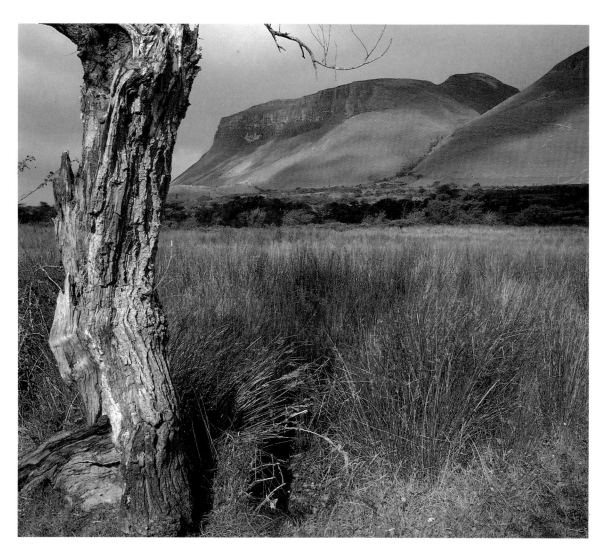

2 *Flora on the Limestone Cliffs*
A wide variety of rare Alpine plants grows on the precipitous slopes of the limestone cliffs. For instance, this is the only site in the British Isles where the fringed sandwort grows. Other plants which thrive in this calcareous environment are mountain avens, alpine saxifrage and maidenhair fern.

3 *A Prehistoric Landscape*
A few miles to the east of here, on a continuation of the gently sloping plateau in County Leitrim, a huge prehistoric landscape of house sites, field systems and burial monuments has been discovered. This whole complex lies under blanket bog at 1300 ft (400 m), compared with present-day settlements which are seldom found higher than 500 ft (150 m). The complex is thought to have been inhabited by Neolithic people 5000 years ago.

Ben Bulbin and the King's Gully

2·13

THE POISONED GLEN
HORSESHOE

STARTING AND FINISHING
POINT
At the hairpin bend on a side-road
off the R251/L82 at Dunlewy
(930192). Dunlewy, to
paraphrase the comment about
Los Angeles in a form appropriate
to this smaller context, is '20
houses in search of a village'.
From the Youth Hostel, drive east
0.9 miles (1.4 km), turning R
here towards an unroofed church
— it is a prominent landmark —
from the R251, whether
travelling east or west. Park at
the hairpin bend near the church.
MAPS
Northern Ireland OS Sheet 1 or
Republic of Ireland Sheet 1 (both
half-inch to the mile) are
adequate. The Glenveagh National
Park one-inch to the mile map
covers the entire route and is
better than either.
LENGTH
7½ miles (12 km)
ASCENT
2800 ft (850 m)

The Poisoned Glen, a morass of ominously green and watery vegetation, is almost surrounded by a line of bare rocky cliffs riven by deep dykes. The circuit of these cliffs is short in distance but not in time as the dykes extend as narrow but steep-sided rocky gaps in the plateau behind the cliffs, thus necessitating much exhilarating but time-consuming descending and climbing. The long views are excellent, dominated across Dunlewy Lough by the fine cone of Errigal which displays sometimes one, sometimes two of its tiny summits, and on a more practical level acts as a useful landmark for navigation.

ROUTE DESCRIPTION (Map 2.13)

From the church *(1)* take the track at the hairpin bend to a bridge 150 yards (135 m) away *(2)*. Cross it, turn L and follow the stream for about a ½ mile (1 km), at which point bogland on the R is a little less wet than further back. Leave the stream half R, striking directly towards Maumlack, carefully crossing the deer fence *(3)* marking entry to Glenveagh National Park on the way. Maumlack (1589 ft/484 m) is topped by an elegant, squared-off cairn. From the summit, walk east to keep to the high ground and then turn R (south) and drop to boggy terrain at Lough Beg. Climb over rough rocky ground to the unnamed peak directly to its south.

Here one enters a region of dykes, about which a general comment may be useful. The choice of route across this pathless region is infinite. However, the closer you are to the cliffs on the R, the harder the dykes are to negotiate — and the more spectacular the scenery. To the L, away from the cliffs, progress is faster but duller. The route described favours the R approach.

Cross the first dyke, climb the rocky promontory beyond it, and cross the second dyke along which the deer fence runs. Luckily the third dyke is also unmistakable because of the string of lenticular little lakes running along it. From this dyke climb steeply through crags, passing rock-bound Lough Maumbeg on

Youth hostel

450

300

Dunlewy Lake

R251/L82

Croloughan L.

① P

STARTING AND
FINISHING
POINT

②

③

Maumlack
△

450

Cronaniv Burn

150

Deer Fence

300

Lough Beg

N

300

Poisoned
Glen

450

450

L.Maumbeg
△
Rocky Cap
North

450

450

450

| 0 | 1 | 2 | 3 Kilometres |
| 0 | 1 | 2 Miles |

Map 2.13 : The Poisoned Glen Horseshoe

The Church at Dunlewy

Opposite: *The Poisoned Glen*

the ascent to the northern summit of Rocky Cap, a peak to the north-east of Slieve Snaght which is unnamed on the maps. This peak has an undulating top so the summit cairn, and there is only one, is useful. (NB If you encounter a second lake on this mountain you are on the way to the southern top and should retrace your steps.)

From Rocky Cap descend north along a spur directly towards Dunlewy (use the church as a target) down steep ground at first, then through a flat and boggy stretch with many tiny lakes, and finally over a surprisingly steep shoulder to the valley floor. Cross the Cronaniv Burn, walking upstream if necessary to ford it, turn L and walk back to the only bridge of the day and the hairpin bend.

1   *The Abandoned Church at Dunlewy*
This Church of Ireland church was built in 1844, but was in full use for only a few years thereafter. After that, one service was held per *year* until 1955 when it was de-roofed and the door walled up. Even in the 1920s Arthur Fox, a scholar from Cambridge, noting that only three families worshipped there, added enigmatically that for that reason he 'would not be over-eager to worship in it'.

2   *The Poisoned Glen*
From along this stretch of the route the glen is unmistakable on the R. The name is said to be derived from the poisonous Irish Splurge (genus Euphoria), which grew along the stream that drains the glen (very ineffectively). However, this explanation is somewhat implausible since it also grew in many other places. The valley is a glacial trough; a glacier originating in the Derryveagh Mountains to the south spilled over the cliffs surrounding the glen before heading first north and then along the lakes to the west of here.

This area was one of the last in which the golden eagle bred; they were still being recorded as late as 1910. Alas, 20 years later eagles had departed from here and from Ireland generally. Some thought has been given recently to attempting to re-introduce them, but it is very likely that this would be unsuccessful as long as farmers continue to use pesticides.

3   *The Deer Fence*
This fence is 28 miles (45 km) long, and thought to be the longest fence in the country. Erected in the 1890s it encloses most, but not all, of the National Park. The herd of 650 red deer which roam within the enclosed area is the largest in Ireland, but it has been introduced, and is not native as in Killarney.

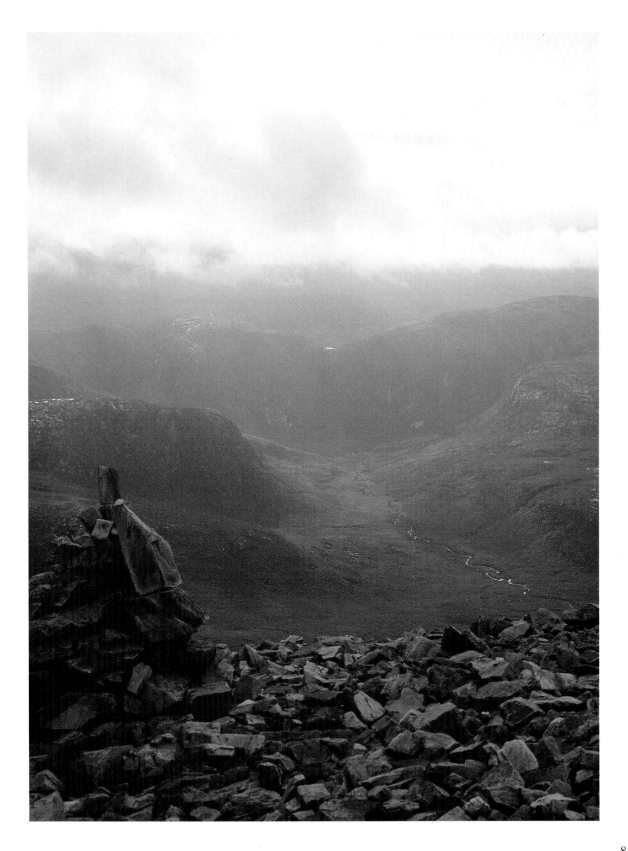

3·14

THE BLUE STACKS

STARTING AND FINISHING
POINT
At the end of a side-road
(973871) off the minor road
circling Lough Eske. The junction
off the minor road is at the
northern end of Lough Eske and is
marked by a 'walking-man' signpost. Park carefully where the side-
road continues as a rough track.
MAPS
The Republic of Ireland OS half-
inch to the mile Sheet 3 is barely
adequate given the complicated
nature of the terrain. The
Northern Ireland OS half-inch to
the mile Sheets 1 and 3 are both
needed to cover the route and are
therefore not recommended.
LENGTH
6½ miles (10.5 km)
ASCENT
1900 ft (580 m)
SAFETY NOTE
Even good maps — and there
aren't any as yet — could not
show the complexity of the
ground over much of this route.
The wet hummocky bogland
slows progress and numerous low
crags cause detours. In addition,
their degree of severity is very
difficult to evaluate in bad
weather. In poor visibility it
would be advisable to go no
further than Lough Belshade, so
keeping to a path (of sorts) all the
way.

The Blue Stacks are a gently moulded, little-frequented range
sheltering shyly behind low foothills near Donegal town. Because
of their boggy surrounds, some might strongly assert that they
are deservedly little-frequented and should remain so. But this
evaluation is a little unfair. This walk takes in small-scale attractive scenery whose prelude and postscript is plain moorland: the
narrow waterfalls that cascade over the foothills of the range, the
rock-rimmed splendour of Lough Belshade, and the expanses of
pink granite slabs facing the summit of Ardnageer. A short but
not easy walk with much variety.

ROUTE DESCRIPTION (Map 3.14)

Walk up the track, the Ulster Way (Donegal) (1), towards the
deep cleft ahead. Where it swings L follow the Way straight
ahead (2) avoiding, or at least postponing, a soggy stretch by
climbing through boulders on its R.

Follow the stream, rejoining the Way for a short distance
further up, into a flat valley which retains water to an unprece-
dented degree even for these watery parts. Noting the large and
distinctive U-bend in the river, continue upstream for a further
130 yards (120 m) and then branch L upstream along a tributary,
taking a subsidiary path, the first, which avoids many hummocks
but which is just as wet as the surrounding hillside.

This path ends at Lough Belshade (3), a high lake bounded on
its further side by magnificent boiler-plate slabs beyond which
rise the rocky undulating mounds of the Blue Stacks. Walk along
the southern shore of the lake (the path, initially intermittent,
soon expires) and then follow the stream issuing into the south-
west corner for a little way before striking north towards
Ardnageer. (A none-too-consoling word about the summits
hereabouts. They are difficult to find because of the numerous
subsidiary summits, and to identify on the maps because few of
them are indicated and fewer still named. The heights are the
surest guide to identification on the maps.)

This stretch towards Ardnageer provides numerous obstacles
to a quick advance. It is a bewildering complex of tiny lakes,
rocky crags, boggy patches, and most memorably great slabs of

smooth, pink granite at all angles from flat to vertical. Beyond this area climb Ardnageer (2061 ft/628 m) which is a distinct rise onto a high, hummocky plateau. There is a summit cairn, but if you are still in doubt watch out for the long slab of white quartzite rock, which is unique in this area and lies 220 yards (200 m) to the west of the summit.

Cross broken ground *(4)* to reach a great wedge of high rocky country stretching south-east between Ardnageer and Croaghgorm, and come gradually off its R (i.e., west) side to avoid the crags at its nose. Descend steeply to Lough Gulladuff, and walk to the R of the stream issuing from it, which is gathering sluggish tributaries here before its precipitous descent by a low waterfall

Map 3.14 : Blue Stacks

Lough Eske from near the start

into lower ground towards Lough Eske. Veer prudently a little way from the stream to avoid small cliffs at the waterfall. Lower down, follow the stream closely to the forestry plantation bounded on its near side by the Ulster Way, up which you toiled earlier. Turn R onto the Way to return to the starting point.

1   The Ulster Way (Donegal)
    This section of the Ulster Way runs from Lough Derg in the south-west of County Donegal to Falcarragh on the north coast, and traverses much of the best of the Donegal highlands. It is 45 miles (75 km) long and is mostly unwaymarked. (A note for those perplexed by the fact that the *Ulster* Way is in the Republic of Ireland: Donegal is in the province of Ulster but not in Northern Ireland. Donegal also extends farther north than any point in Northern Ireland.)

2   Hydro-electricity on the Corabber River
    If rivers are to be harnessed for electricity this scheme shows the way to do it. Water is stored unobtrusively at Lough Belshade. A pipe runs underground below the steep slope under your feet, parallel to the Corabber River, and the power-house is hidden in the forestry plantation passed earl-

Lough Belshade

ier, on the ascent. There is virtually no disturbance beyond the end of the track, which is a little way upstream. During construction, much of the heavy equipment was flown in by helicopter to avoid extending the track for lorries.

3   *The Treasures of Lough Belshade*
The Gaelic form of this name, 'Loch bel sead,' means 'the lake of the jewel'. This is thought to refer to an incident in 1593 when English troops captured the Abbey in Donegal. Before they arrived the monks fled, taking with them the treasures of the Abbey which they hid on an island in Lough Belshade — unfortunately no one knows which.

4   *The Crashed Plane*
A British war-plane crashed in the valley north of here in World War II and its wreckage can still be seen near a narrow stream. During the war, planes based in Northern Ireland just to the east of here headed for the North Atlantic over the narrow neck of neutral Irish Free State territory (as the Republic was then called) with the secret agreement of the Irish government. This avoided a lengthy detour round the north of Donegal. This plane, a Sunderland flying-boat on a reconnaissance mission, crashed killing six of its crew.

Loading bays

⑥

Promontory

⑤

Building

Small
Cairn ④ Trig obelisk

Amphitheatre

To N56

Finish of
Long Route

L. Naboll

Loading bays

Muckish

300

450   600

450

Scree

300

Falcarragh

Shrine

Finish of
Medium
Route

Crocknalaragagh

Glenveagh

③

0   1   2   3 *Kilometres*

0   1   2 *Miles*

<u>Map 4.15</u> : Errigal to Muckish

N

L. Aluirg

Aghla Beg
South

300

L. Feeane

Aghla Mt.

450

450

300

Altan Lough

300

L. Nabehy

Stepping stones

Joey Glover
Memorial

Macoght

450

Route to
Finish of Short Route

Scree

Errigal △

②

600

①

450

300

To Glenveagh

Altan Farm
Pillars

R251/L82   STARTING AND FINISHING POINT

ERRIGAL TO MUCKISH

STARTING POINT
On the R251/L82 east of
Dunlewy at 940196. Drive 2.6
miles (4.2 km) east from the
Youth Hostel and park at a
walking signpost on the L
featuring a startlingly buxom
wench. If driving west, watch out
for the gate pillars labelled 'Altan
Farm' on the R and park at the
signpost a ½ mile (1 km) further
on.

FINISHING POINTS
For the short route: At the starting
point above.
For the medium route: At Muckish
Gap (999269), at a shrine on the
highest point of an unclassified
road running south-east from
Falcarragh to Glenveagh. ·
For the long route: At the end of a
side-road off the N56 (008302).
Take the N56 west from
Creeslough for 1.8 miles
(2.9 km), then turn L onto the
side-road (if coming from the
other direction turn R just beyond
the cemetery on the L of the
road). Drive straight ahead for
3.6 miles (5.8 km) and park
where the metalled road ends.

MAPS
Northern Ireland OS Sheet 1 or
Republic of Ireland OS Sheet 1
(both half-inch to the mile). The
first half of the route is also on the
Glenveagh National Park one inch
to the mile map.

Though they are otherwise sharply contrasted, Errigal and
Muckish have this much in common: they are easily recognized.
In fact, they are two of the most easily recognized mountains in
Ireland. They do not have much else in common. Errigal is a
graceful quartzite cone with long scree slopes falling from a tiny
double summit. Muckish is a long, gently sloping upland, a rock-
strewn plateau standing high and conspicuous above the surrounding hills and low boglands.

Their locations, aloof from other high mountains, make it a
little difficult to provide good looped walks encompassing each
of them separately. The solution is to combine them in a long
south-west to north-east walk also taking in two of the Aghlas, a
fine trio of peaks that lie between them.

This is the route of the Joey Glover Marathon (see p. 93)
except that the marathon goes north-east to south-west. The
advantage of walking in the direction given here is that it allows
an early 'out' for the faint-hearted, *after* the finest peak —
Errigal — has been climbed (a second drop-out point at Muckish
Gap is also indicated) and, no trivial consideration, it means that
the strong prevailing westerlies are behind the walker.

It is hardly necessary to add that the coastal and mountain
views on this route are superb and the underfoot terrain mostly
(but not wholly) good. All that — and two options to drop out,
should you be so foolish as to take either of them.

ROUTE DESCRIPTION (Map 4.15)

Take the rough path across bogland towards Errigal following
posts where the path is indistinct. At drier, steeper ground
where the posts cease, follow the clear path upwards to a small
cairn on a mound (useful later on in the route). Higher up climb,
with steep scree on the R, to the Joey Glover memorial pillar *(1)*.
Walk onward from here along a narrow path with ground
falling steeply on both sides to the first summit of Errigal
(2466 ft/752 m), which has the foundations of an OS obelisk. The
second summit at about the same height is 30 yards (27 m) further on, reached by a narrow path. These are reputed to be the
smallest summits in Ireland, a claim few would dispute. The

LENGTH

$6\frac{1}{2}$ miles (9.5 km) for the short route: 9 miles (14.5 km) for the medium route; 12 miles (19 km) for the long route

ASCENT

2800 ft (850 m) for the short route; 4800 ft (1460 m) for the medium route; 6100 ft (1860 m) for the long route

SAFETY NOTE

The full walk is long with strenuous climbing, so an early start is essential. The cliffs and scree slopes at Mackoght and the Aghlas are not well represented on the maps, but are easy to avoid. The descent from Muckish requires your full attention at a time, late in a long day, when attention may be flagging.

---

views, especially towards the Derryveagh Mountains, are superb.

Retrace your steps as far as the small cairn mentioned above, and strike out from here to the L *(2)* to Mackoght (about 1600 ft/500 m) across rough, pathless country broken by occasional avoidable rocky outcrops. From Mackoght the next goal is the R-hand (i.e., eastern) end of Altan Lough. Bear R of the direct line to avoid cliffs and scree on the north-east side of Mackoght and also to avoid a shelving bogland, gentle on this side but craggy and steep where it overlooks the lough. The lough marks the first decision point.

Short route Take the clear grassy track on the near side of the stream entering the lough, walk to the R251/L82 at Altan Farm pillars, turn R and walk to the starting point.

Medium route If you wish to continue, cross the stepping-stones at the stream entering the lough, and with the curious castle-like derelict building on the L climb Aghla Mor keeping initially close to the lake to avoid a small drop further up on the direct route. Aghla Mor (1916 ft/581 m) — the alternative name 'Wee Errigal' might be more appropriately applied to Mackoght — has scree slopes to north-east and south-west and these come close together towards the summit to give a fine hogsback peak.

With these scree slopes in mind, retrace your steps a little and then descend steeply to the peat hags on the south side of Lough Feeane, and walk along the broad saddle south of the lake. Climb through the boulder field to the more southern (of two) Aghla Begs (about 1900 ft/580 m). From here swing slightly R of the direct approach again, to reach the south side of Lough Aluirg where there is but a narrow passable strip between the lake on the L and the forestry plantation on the R.

The next section poses a navigational problem. The hummocky, wet high ground to the north-east contains an indistinct peak, Crocknalaragagh, and three lakes, which are better navigational landmarks than the mountain. Across the entire area runs a meandering fence which, if it remains as it is at present, leads to the central lake. But will it? Perhaps it will collapse, be moved or be augmented by other fences, so leading to errors. The best plan is probably to rely on one's own resources. Aim for the small area between the two eastern lakes by climbing steeply at first and then walking over flat boggy ground. Ignoring Crocknalaragagh, walk between the two lakes and climb a little to gain a distinct ridge (it has forest further down, close on its R) that runs all the way down to Muckish Gap *(3)*. This is the second drop-out point and marks the end of the medium route.

Long route If you intend to complete the long walk cross the road, go round to the L of the mound which shelters the shrine to take the rough path which ascends a spur terminating about 1000 ft (300 m) above on Muckish plateau. Walk across the gently sloping plateau, keeping to its south-east edge to avoid rocky ground, to reach the OS obelisk marking the summit *(4)*.

The next task, an essential one, is to find the way down, which both here and at the quarry below requires you to keep to paths that give a safe way down the rough steep ground. From the obelisk head west for about 220 yards (200 m) to a small cairn and follow a faint path half R which originates about here and bends L over a promontory bounded by cliffs and steep ground to R and L.

This path ends at the quarry, which takes the form of a small semi-amphitheatre in a spot likely to excite considerable awe *(5)*. It consists of a tiny sandy plain, rusting mining artifacts and curious light-brown towers fronting the partly man-made cliffs which half surround the quarry. The only sound, as likely as not, is the harsh caw of the ravens fluttering overhead.

Let not awe cause a hasty descent. Walk to the ruined building at the centre of the rim of the quarry and take the miners' path which is to its R (facing out) and to the L of a small stream. The path follows stumps of iron fence posts and decayed wood poles which occasionally peter out. In case of doubt, remember that the path runs wholly *between* two streams and crosses a sand run at *one* point only *(6)*.

At a tiny valley on level ground, clogged with discarded rocks, cross the stream on the R and descend steeply and directly to the loading bays visible below. Take the grassy quarry road which begins at the bays, climbing the boulders across it a little way down to follow the clear rocky quarry road below them to a metalled road, where the route finishes.

The Joey Glover Memorial, Errigal

1 *The Joey Glover Memorial*
   The simple cairn and plaque here are in memory of Joey Glover, a great mountaineering enthusiast, whose special love was for these, his local mountains. He was murdered in 1976 by the Provisional IRA in one of their many 'mistakes'.

2 *Drumlin Country*
   The curious cluster of tiny oval hills seen to the L on the low ground between Errigal and Mackoght appears to be drumlins formed by the passage of moving ice. Most are grassed, but this cluster is of rough stone.

3 *Muckish Gap*
   This is a glacial breach, the most spectacular of several along the line of mountains from Errigal to Muckish. The col was once 400 ft (120 m) higher, but ice moving north from the Derryveagh mountains broke through the low point here to form this impressive gap.

The route from Errigal

4   *The Disappointments of Caesar Otway*

Caesar Otway, the splendidly named intrepid Victorian traveller, climbed Muckish in the 1820s. After four hours (sic!) exertion he neared the top. 'I ran, covered with perspiration and panting with heat, to mount the topmost ridge; and just as we arrived there . . . and began to feast on the immense vision of the earth and ocean beneath us, a vast murky cloud from the Atlantic, big with sleet and moisture, enveloped us as well as the whole top of the mountain as with a night-cap, and made every thing so dark, indistinct, and dreary, that we could scarcely see one another.'

Some things never change.

5   *The Mine Workings of Muckish*

Fine-quality white quartzite sand (99.5 per cent silica) used in the manufacture of spectacles, was mined here until 1955, when the workings became uneconomic. The path to the upper workings used by the miners was obviously well made, but is now ruined.

6   *The Letterkenny and Burtonport Extension railway*

The grassy embankments marking the route of this disused line can be clearly seen on the descent. The L&BER was a narrow-gauge railway running from Letterkenny in a meandering curve to the town of Burtonport on the west coast of Donegal, and was primarily intended as a means of developing the fishing industry there. The route was a difficult one. — mostly unyielding granite rock — or, equally difficult, too-easily yielding soft bogland. Opened in 1903, the line closed in 1940.

Introduction

The mountains of the West, that is, of the counties of Galway (pre-eminently), Mayo and Clare, are located in small, distinct groups separated by low passes and long valleys. Access is good, given the scattered nature of habitation which clings to the narrow fringe between ocean, bogland and mountain. From Clifden, the core area to the east is but a short drive away so the roads, though generally poor, do not have to be endured for very great distances.

The most obvious characteristic that all these discrete mountain ranges have in common is that, to use an Irishism, they are all different! Bleak, flat, boggy upland, limestone terraces, fine rocky conical peaks, upland plateaux with cliffy flanks, grassy hills ending in sea-cliffs, are all represented here. This meant that the selection of routes was quite simple. What was required was just one route in each of the best ranges coupled with a firm resolve not to include that almost as good or nearly as satisfying *second* route in each range. The routes therefore almost chose themselves.

The one range where it was most tempting to choose a second route was the Twelve Bens. What a bewitching magical group — a tiny but crowded canvas of conical peaks in bare rocky splendour, soaring skyward so that it is almost impossible to accept that the highest peak is less than 2400 ft (730 m) high. The route chosen is the most spectacular classic.

The Maamturks lie just across the Inagh valley from the Bens. To quote a well-used and observant phrase: they are the Bens straightened out and with the tops sheared off. It is indeed true that the tops barely rise above a rocky quartzite plateau and that the range more or less orients itself in a narrow line. This latter characteristic makes good circuits almost impossible to devise. With this limitation in mind, a route has been chosen to one of the cols that cause such anguish to those hardy souls doing a full traverse of the range, with a return along the Western Way.

There are two routes for potterers, both in very distinct areas just south of the fiord of Killary Harbour, the great divide between Connemara (western Galway) and the mountains of Mayo. A stroll along the fiord, all of it on path or track, is navigationally easy and scenically a delightful juxtaposition of coast and hillside. The other walk is only a few miles away in the Benchoonas, an unfrequented, unpretentious shaggy group of hills with great geological diversity and simply staggering long-distance views — a great area for carefree wandering.

Doo Lough and Mweelrea

North across Killary Harbour is Mweelrea, at a modest 2688 ft (819 m) the highest mountain in the entire area. The Mweelrea massif, for Mweelrea is one of a group of hills rising from a plateau, is the best of three ranges, sectors of a great circle of mountains split by north-south and centre to east passes. Of the several routes considered onto the summit plateau (including one by boat across Killary!) this one traverses the rim of the corrie cleaving the eastern side of the massif. A memorable excursion that, like some of the others, almost chose itself.

Finally, on the outskirts of the West two greatly contrasting walks: Achill Island provides a comparatively easily accessible cliff walk in an area which has many that are far from accessible — and it also happens to be one of the most memorable; the Burren is unique in Ireland — a strange area of limestone slabs which shelters a bewildering range of rare and varied flora.

Mention should perhaps be made of Croagh Patrick, a notable omission. Croagh Patrick is Ireland's 'holy' mountain, an attribute which has blighted it with an ugly scar of a pilgrimage track and squat chapel on the summit. It is probably better to leave it to the penitential multitudes, and seek spiritual solace on unspoilt and less-frequented hills.

1·16

KILLARY HARBOUR

STARTING AND FINISHING
POINT
At Killary Harbour Youth Hostel
(769651) in Rosroe on the
southern shore of the fiord. From
Leenane take the N59 towards
Clifden turning R after 4.4 miles
(7.0 km) (this is the *second* side-
turn within a few hundred yards
on a road which has no side-roads
on this side after Leenane.)
Continue along the length of
Lough Fee and 0.2 miles (350 m)
beyond it fork R uphill. The
Hostel is 1.8 miles (3.0 km)
further on. The approach road is
in poor condition; almost as much
pot-hole and dirt track as it is
tarmac.
MAP
The 1:50 000 Connemara map is
recommended. The OS half-inch
to the mile Sheet 10 suffices.
LENGTH
5 miles (8 km)
ASCENT
400 ft (120 m)

This is an easy walk nearly all of which is on a clear path or track
with little climbing. The route is along the shore of a narrow
fiord, by far Ireland's best (though some would say that it is
Ireland's *only* true fiord). Across the waters the great southern
wall of Mweelrea rises unbroken from shore to summit, 2600 ft
(800 m) of grassy slopes. A good walk for a day of low cloud, but
nonetheless it would be a pity to miss the full glory of the excellent sea and mountain scenery.

ROUTE DESCRIPTION (Map 1.16)

Walk along the road away from the Hostel *(1)* and the tiny harbour beside it, turning L onto a track just before the first house
on the L. Follow this upwards ignoring the gate on the L set in a
stone wall which runs beside the track for a short distance. A
little further on, Killary Harbour *(2)* is fully revealed. Look out
on the opposite shore for the remains of a pre-famine village *(3)*.

Route-finding from here is simple, with one proviso vital for
the return. Watch out for the deserted house (rough definition: a
deserted house is roofed, a ruin is not) half-hidden in rhododendron, and note also the lateral gated wall beyond it. Between
house and wall search carefully for a green track heading back.
Though barely more than a gently sloping stretch of grass amidst
steeply rising ground, it is a stretch of grass that runs surrepti-
tiously slightly uphill and almost parallel to the good track that
you are on. Note this for the return carefully.

For now, continue along the coast, cross a concrete bridge
over a stream which descends briskly as a series of low waterfalls
(a good place for a picnic) and pass the ruin on the L, the first on
the fiord side. Around here the south-east outlier of Mweelrea
descends in a diminuendo of rocky hillocks into Killary and the
end of the Maamturks increasingly dominates the skyline beyond
it. On the near side, old scattered oaks shelter in a slight hollow
ahead.

There is nothing to stop further onward wandering, but the
best of the scenery is behind. For the return take the track L
already noted, and follow it to near a deserted house set at right
angles to the shore. Just before this house the track inexplicably,

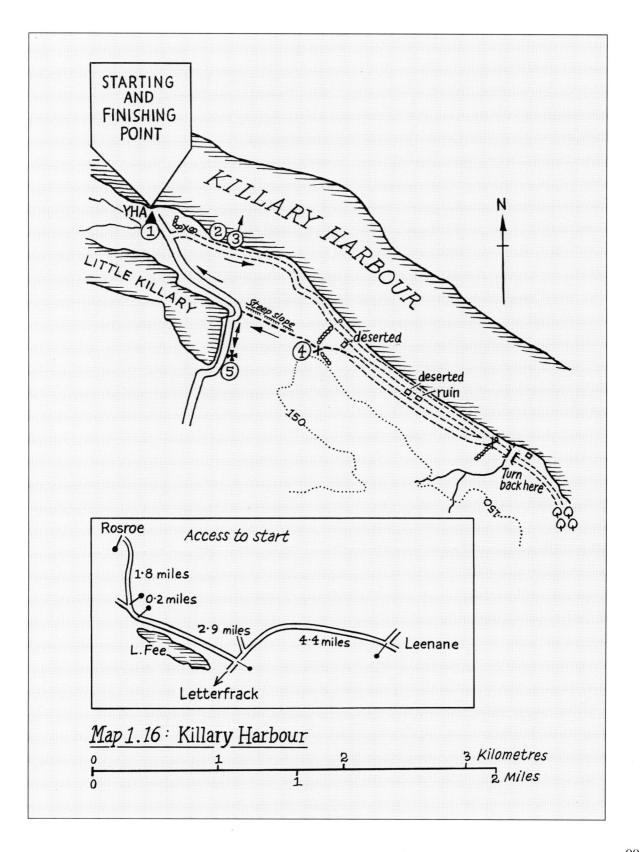

Map 1.16 : Killary Harbour

Killary Harbour Youth Hostel

but fortunately only temporarily expires at a wall that must be crossed. Beyond the house it resumes resolutely uphill, no longer meekly paralleling its coastal companion. The path ends at a corner in a stone wall. Take a gate on the L here and follow the fence beyond steeply uphill along a curious rocky escarpment *(4)* running close by on the R. At the crest the delightful Little Killary Harbour comes into view. From here continue steeply downhill to the road.

At the road turn L to visit the tiny Church of Ireland church *(5)* tucked in behind a high wall on the L a few hundred yards away. Afterwards retrace your steps to the starting point.

1   *A Philosopher at Killary*
    The Youth Hostel was the temporary home of the philosopher Ludwig Wittgenstein after World War II (of course it was not a hostel then). Here he wrote his book *Philosophical Investigations*.

2   *Killary Fiord*
    During the Ice Age, a glacier pushed its way out to sea hereabouts along an existing river valley, deepening it from a shallow V to the deep U of the present-day fiord and leaving a bar at the entrance, the equivalent of a moraine. The fiord is deeper at the landward end.

Opposite: The shoreline at Killary

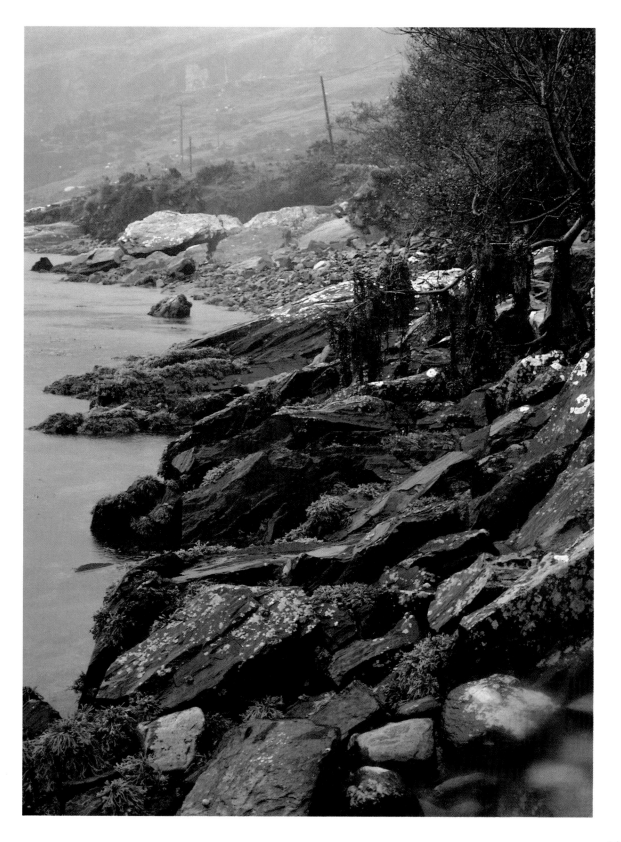

The shelter provided by the hills and the unusually deep water in the harbour have made it a centre for mussel farming. The mussels cling to long ropes hanging from the rafts. Apart from being unsightly, questions have recently been asked about the chemical effects of this type of intensive fish-farming.

3 *A Pre-famine Village*

The pre-famine village across the fiord and clearly visible from this side was called Uggool. Tillage beds climb the steep and infertile hill behind the village, indicating how desperate the plight of the land-starved peasants was in the 1830s and 1840s.

4 *The Escarpment*

The curious cliff and trench here was caused by the rubbing of a chain which the devil was pulling to drag away Saint Roc, a local holy man. If that is too difficult to believe, the alternative explanation is that it is a thrust fault caused by the movement of one body of rock relative to a contiguous body. (How dull science is compared to popular theology!)

5 *The Church at Salrock*

The small Church of Ireland church maintained a curious custom in the past. Mourners at funerals smoked clay pipes after the religious service and these were heaped in the graveyard. Two plaques on the inside wall remember two brothers, both born during World War I and killed in World War II. It must have been a heavy sacrifice not only for their parents, but for the tiny Protestant community of the area.

Killary Harbour and Mweelrea

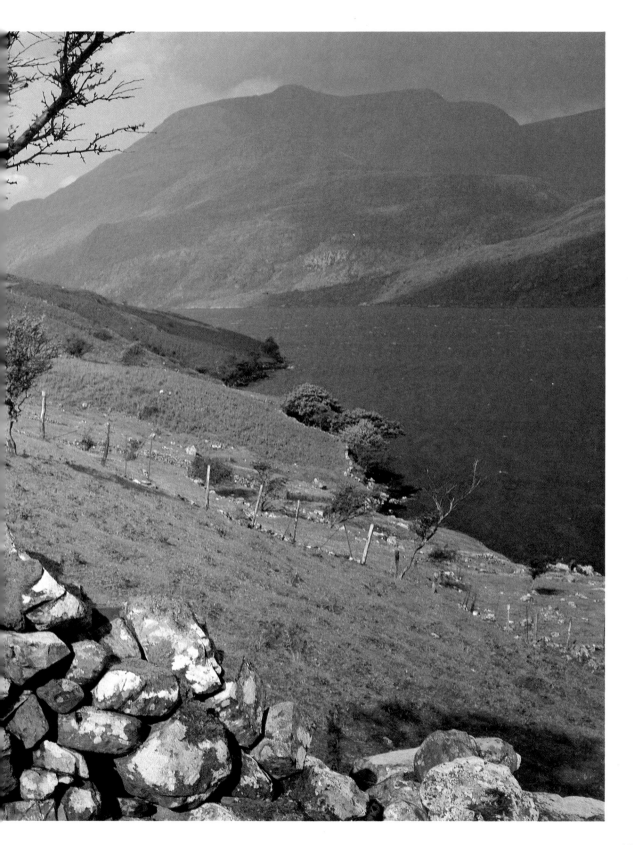

1·17

ACHILL HEAD

STARTING AND FINISHING POINT
Keem Bay (560045) at the western end of Achill Island. Take the N59 to Mulrany and there take the R319/L141 to Dooagh. Continue onwards to the road head at Keem Bay where there are several large car-parks. Leave plenty of time for the drive as the roads are generally poor.

MAPS
The OS half-inch to the mile Sheet 6 is the only contoured map available. A local guide *Achill Island* (published by Bob Kingston) is in the form of a map on a scale of 1.9 in to the mile. Although it has no contours it is quite useful.

LENGTH
5 miles (8 km)

ASCENT
1100 ft (340 m)

Achill (pronounced '*Ack-ill*') is the largest island off the coast, though its insular status is impaired as it is joined to the mainland by a road-bridge. The island is shaped like a right-angled triangle, its most acute angle at Achill Head jutting out defiantly west into the Atlantic. Sea-cliffs dominate the two sides near this angle, low to the west of Keem Bay where the walk starts but rising to nearly 2200 ft (670 m) under the summit of Croaghaun Mountain further north. Between Keem and Achill Head the walk takes in some of the most breath-taking sea-cliff scenery in Ireland. Although the route does not include Croaghaun, the sweep of cliffs under that mountain can be seen clearly from Achill Head — ironically they cannot be seen from Croaghaun itself.

ROUTE DESCRIPTION (Map 1.17)

Before starting it might be of interest to consider the surroundings. Keem Bay is tucked into a bowl of mountains unbroken except for the ocean and the coastal strip whence you drove *(1)*. The curious aspect is that nearly the entire sweep of hills around is 'one-sided': the sides hidden from here terminate abruptly either in sea-cliffs or corrie wall. Thus the surroundings uncannily mirror St Kilda, far west of Scotland in the Atlantic.

From the bay *(2)* climb over pathless grass to the top of Moyteoge Head to the south-west, which is crowned by the look-out post clearly visible from the bay. Once there navigation is easy. Turn R and walk north-west towards and over the two great waves of rising ground ahead which fall on the L to the sea in dramatic sea-cliffs. As you advance, the bulky but dull shoulder of Croaghaun (2192 ft/668 m) increasingly dominates the view. A little further on, the high but not sheer cliffs falling from its summit to the sea with the curve of the Belmullet peninsula behind, can be clearly seen. In spite of their height these cliffs are not as impressive as the Achill Head sea-cliffs to the L and further on also to the R.

The cliffs on Achill Head converge gradually to a knife-edge and conditions on the day (for example, wind and the slipperiness of the rocks) combined with the walker's burgeoning fear of an

Map 1.17 : Achill Head

unscheduled visit to the slowly pounding sea far below will
eventually dictate a retreat. When prudence advises, turn back
and initially retrace your steps, with the cliffs now on the R.
Where feasible, descend gradually L from the cliffs, walk
upstream roughly parallel to a westward-flowing stream *(3)*
below on the L and, when they come into view, head to two
small lakes at the col between the Achill Head cliffs R and the
rising featureless flank of Croaghaun L *(4)*.

From these lakes continue in roughly the same direction
(south-east) to pick up a stream, noting at the start of this stretch
the distinctive cone of Croagh Patrick ahead neatly framed by
Croaghaun and Moyteoge Head. Follow this stream downhill
back to the car-park at Keem, passing on the way two imposing
ruins *(5)* and an equally imposing deserted house, the latter the
old coastguard station.

1   Amethysts at Keem Bay
On the last ridge on the road into Keem, amethysts were
discovered in the 1960s in the course of constructing the
present road to the bay. The clear purple gemstone can still
be found with a little patient searching.

2   *Shark fishing at Keem Bay*
Keem Bay was a centre for the shark-fishing industry for 25 years up to the mid-1970s. Basking sharks up to 35 ft (10 m) long and weighing up to 6 tons (tonnes) were caught in nets attached to the cliffs and were then killed by harpoon from curraghs, the fragile row-boats traditional on the Atlantic coast. It must have been a gory business. Only the sharks' liver oil and fins were used, the latter being exported to the Far East.

Achill coastline with Achill Head in the distance

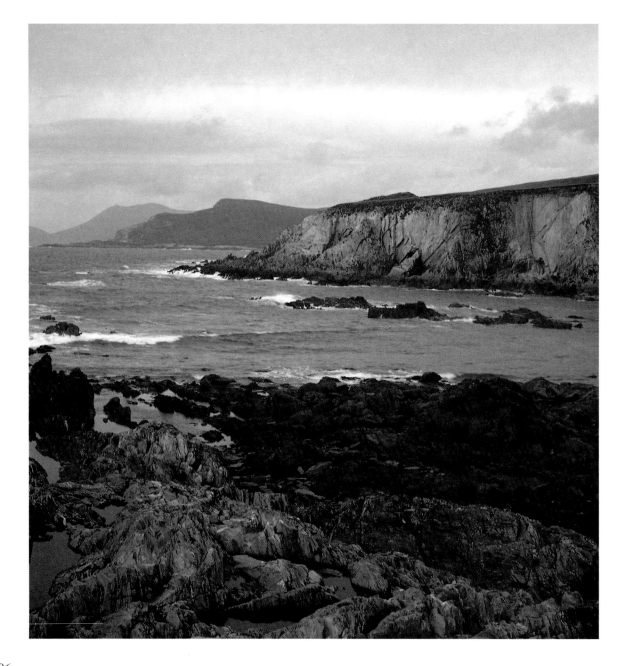

3   *Booleys*

The oval, stone-wall enclosures along this stream are good examples of *booleys*, shelters which cattle-minders inhabited in the summers while their bovine charges grazed on the summer pastures. Achill is the last place in Ireland where this practice survived. The context in which this practice occurred is described on p.15.

4   *The Views of Eric Newby*

Eric Newby, the noted English travel-writer, climbed Croaghaun in his youth. Many years later, as described in his book, *Round Ireland in Slow Gear*, he climbed it again. He had exactly the same view on the two occasions — zero visibility caused by low cloud — so it is unlikely that even the not-easily-discouraged Newby will ever come to believe in third time lucky.

5   *Captain Boycott*

These ruins, a substantial house and store, were built around 1857 by Captain Boycott, a local landlord. He later moved east to the Mayo mainland where he achieved unwanted fame by becoming the original victim of the effective protest action named after him.

Keem Bay

THE BENCHOONAS

At the car-park of Kylemore
Abbey (748585) on the northern
side of the N59, 2½ miles (4 km)
east of Letterfrack and 9½ miles
(15 km) west of Leenane. The
Abbey is well signposted and its
imposing pile is clearly visible
from the Leenane direction.
MAPS
The Connemara 1:50 000 map is
recommended. The OS half-inch
to the mile Sheet 10 is barely
adequate.
LENGTH
5½ miles (9 km)
ASCENT
2950 ft (900 m)

This modest and little-known range provides one of the most
scenic grandstands in Ireland, a stupendous mix of mountain and
ocean. Mweelrea, the Maamturks, the Bens and the island-
spattered ocean in turn drawing the eye full circle. While it
boasts no 'classic' conical peaks, all its tops being quite mundane
and some even downright shapeless, two are remarkable in other
ways. Duaghruagh/Duchruach is a shaggy little mountain, all
rough rocky hillocks and lochans, which bears a remarkable
resemblance to the much better-known Haystacks in the Lake
District. Altnagaighera/Binn Fhraoigh is simply a narrow spur
but its grassy top is crowned and its western prow guarded by
extraordinary, conglomerate crags. An easy walk of continuously
changing interests.

ROUTE DESCRIPTION (Map 2.18)

Leaving the car-park turn L, walk resolutely L round the back of
the tea-room, whose delights should be reserved for the return,
and continue along the tidy track beyond it to the T-junction.
Turn R here and look out immediately for the sign proclaiming
'The Way to the Statue of the Sacred Heart'. Walk as directed,
zigzagging upward through dense rhododendrons that allow only
brief, tantalizing glimpses of the Abbey. The occasional crosses
along here mark the Stations, a Roman Catholic devotional exer-
cise — not a physical one as you might surmise from the slope.

At the statue abandon the path — it is about to abandon you
— and head diagonally L uphill to the summit of Doughruagh
(1756 ft/529 m) avoiding the occasional easily avoidable crag.
(The only reason for the diagonal rather than the direct approach
is to give a slightly more satisfactory route.) As implied above, it
is well worth allowing time to potter round the hillocks and
lochans of the summit. Incidentally, if a return at this point is
necessary, head straight back to the Sacred Heart to avoid
becoming enmeshed in impenetrable undergrowth if the path
down from the statue is missed.

From the summit, marked by a cairn and a fence post (no
fence), the aim is to descend to the R of the small lake in the

valley between Doughruagh and Altnagaighera. Take an initial swing L of the direct line; the direct descent is steep and rocky, though the recommended route is not all that much better. The lake, Lough na Crapai, is warmed by a thermal spring, which may be an extra inducement if you are contemplating a swim. If you just want a stop for a bite to eat and a rest, the area close to the small waterfalls on the inlet stream is ideal.

The steep wall of grass rising opposite to the top of Altnagaighera is the next goal. First head diagonally L up the slope towards the nose on the west of the summit. Climb through one of several gullies in the conglomerate ramparts to emerge on the long, narrow summit ridge of Altnagaighera (1791 ft/546 m) on which squat the curious 'pudding stone' knolls and a tiny lake.

Map 2.18:

The Benchoonas

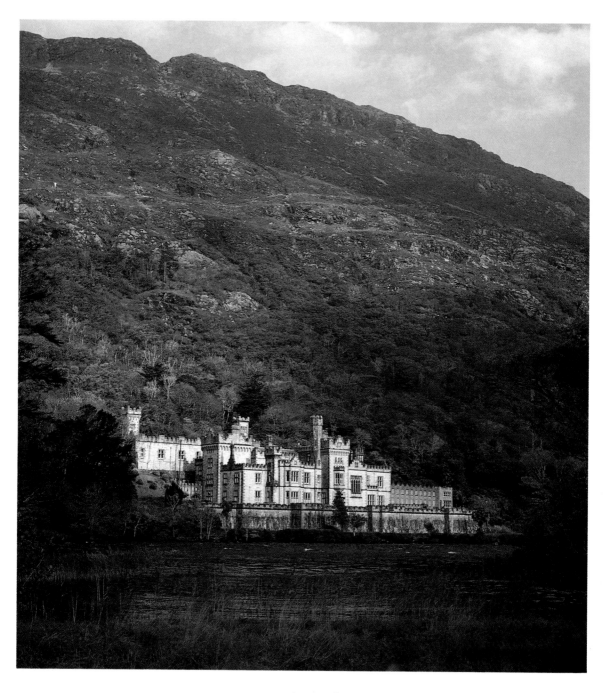

Kylemore Abbey and Doughruagh

From Altnagaighera onward, the underfoot conditions are a trifle anti-climactic, a dull, heaving bogland, though the views remain superb. Climb Garraun/Maolchnoc (1973 ft, 602 m), the highest peak in the Benchoonas. From here retrace your steps a short way along the broad, soggy ridge south-west, and then turn south to point 523 m. Continue south from point 523 m, picking up the R bank of a stream which flows south-east into Kylemore

The Benchoonas from Letterfrack

Lough. When the road (the N59) is first seen, veer a little R of the stream to avoid enclosed fields near a farm. However, do not venture too far R on this descent as thick rhododendron bushes and small but nasty crags fronting the lake form an impenetrable barrier.

Turn R onto the road and walk for ½ mile (1 km) along a lovely stretch of road with Kylemore Lough close on the L, the steeply rising slopes of Doughruagh on the R. Go through the gate on the R where the road veers L, and walk along the track beyond it, which is hemmed in by rhododendron bushes and an oakwood *(1)*. Walk past Kylemore Chapel, the Abbey *(2)* and finally enter the tea-rooms, a visit which will by now have been well merited.

1   *The Rhododendron*

The rhododendron, which boasts such beautiful flowers every June, is the bane of the oakwoods. A native of Turkey and the Himalayas, it flourished in Ireland before the Ice Age. The cold killed it off here and it remained east of the Black Sea until 1800, when it was introduced. Unfortunately it is now back with a vengeance and thrives in areas with acid soils, where it chokes other plants and is extraordinarily difficult to eradicate.

2   *Kylemore Abbey and Chapel*

The gothic pile of Kylemore Abbey, set into the oakwoods above Kylemore Lough, was built in the nineteenth century by a wealthy Liverpool merchant and passed into the hands of the Benedictine nuns in 1921. The Chapel to the east of the main house is a replica of Norwich Cathedral. The Abbey is now an international boarding school for girls.

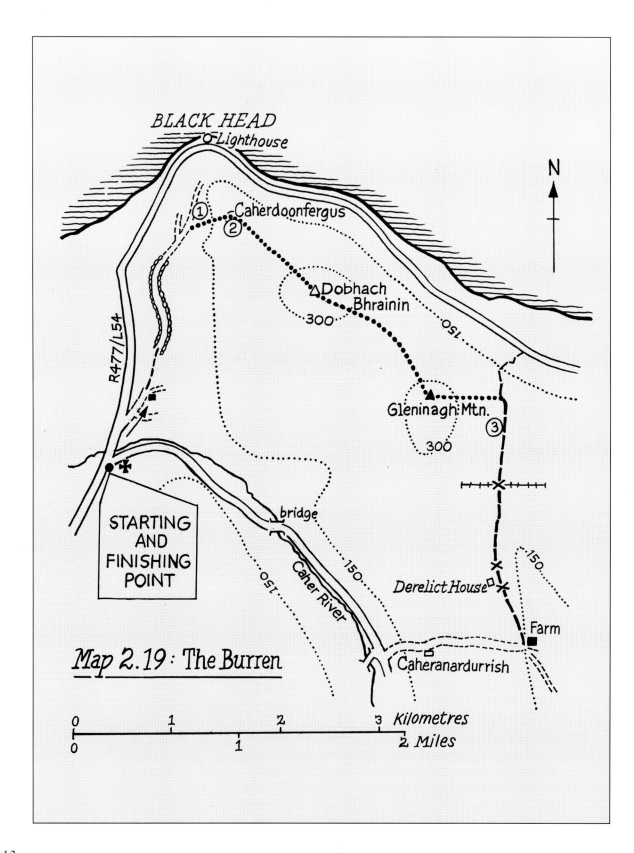

BLACK HEAD

Lighthouse

N

① Caherdoonfergus
②

△ Dobhach
Bhrainin

300

R477/L54

150

▲ Gleninagh Mtn.
③

300

STARTING
AND
FINISHING
POINT

bridge

150

Caher River

150

Derelict House □

150

Farm ■

Map 2.19 : The Burren

Caheranardurrish

| 0 | | 1 | | 2 | | 3 | *Kilometres* |
| 0 | | | 1 | | | 2 | *Miles* |

2·19

THE BURREN

STARTING AND FINISHING
POINT
At or near the side-turn off the
R477/L54 at Fanore (144088).
MAPS
T. D. Robinson's stylish and
artistic map *The Burren*, on a scale
of 1:35 200 (1.8 in to the mile),
while otherwise unsurpassed, is
uncontoured. The alternative is
the OS half-inch to the mile Sheet
14.
LENGTH
$9\frac{1}{2}$ miles (15 km)
ASCENT
1500 ft (460 m)

The Burren of north-west Clare, 60 square miles (160 square
km) of karstic country, is quite unlike any other in Ireland. From
a distance the hills, which rarely rise over 1000 ft (300 m), look
like a pile of stacked grey plates, each smaller than the one below
it. Close up, the landscape is almost lunar, a set of platforms
composed of flat slabs of limestone broken by long, narrow
grooves called grikes. Each platform ends in a short cliff above
which is another grey platform.

The botanic and archaeological variety of the Burren matches
its scenic weirdness. Plants of widely diverse origins thrive in the
lime-rich patches of soil, or shelter in the narrow crevices of the
grikes. Sites from many eras from Stone Age to medieval dot the
hills.

In such an area the walker might prefer to wander freely
rather than be constricted by a formal walk. The walk given here
has at least the virtue of providing most of the elements which
make the Burren what it is: the limestone terraces and cliffs, the
varied flora and archaeology, the excellent coastal views of
Galway Bay and beyond, as well as commonplace fields and quiet
country roads.

ROUTE DESCRIPTION (Map 2.19)

Walk north, that is, with the coast on the L, along the coast road,
the R477/L54 and turn first R up a track. Where the track swings
sharply R at a bungalow on the R, turn L off it along a wisp of a
path. Continue roughly on the level as it improves to a wide track
between stone walls that rises gradually across the hillside. Cross
three stone walls (carefully) on this almost imperceptible ascent
and after the third, where the track divides, take the R branch.
Turn R off it after a short distance *(1)* where it levels off, so
heading directly and pathlessly for the great ring-fort of Caherdoonfergus *(2)* across the limestone pavements.

From the ringfort head directly to Dobhach Bhrainin
(1045 ft/319 m), climbing several terraces on the way (this is a
constant feature until after Gleninagh). The top is marked by a
small cairn, a useful edifice in flat terrain. Descend to the pass
towards Gleninagh Mountain so avoiding grassy hollows on the

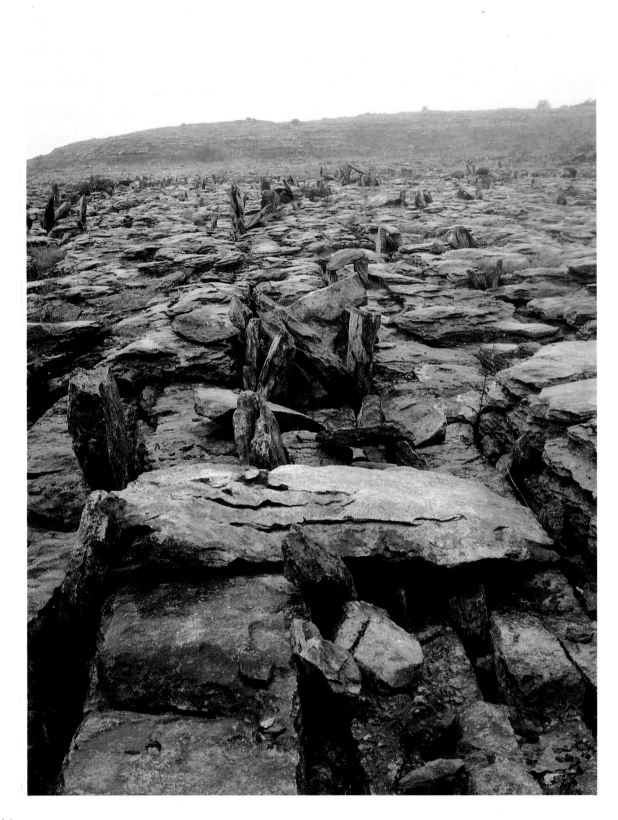

direct route, and ascend directly to Gleninagh, which is exactly the same height as Dobhach Bhrainin, and is marked by a stubby OS obelisk.

Descend to the pass to the east and at it turn R along a track that is difficult to find at the pass itself but is clear a little way down. This track deteriorates to a path through fields in the high grassy Gleninagh South valley *(3)*, scrub and limestone slabs on both sides. Cross a wall and at the gate just beyond, where you may by now have concluded that the path is purely imaginary, head towards a derelict house visible to the R of the valley, picking up the path again closer to it. Take the good track which originates at the house to what appears to be a crossroad (though the L branch terminates at a nearby farm) and turn R uphill here along another track, passing Caheranardurrish, reputedly a sheeben and church, just over the crest.

Descend on a winding course, still on the track, to a metalled road. Turn R onto it and walk steadily downhill all the way to the coast road.

Grikes

1   *Flora of the Limestone Slabs*

Bloody cranesbill, mountain avens and spring gentians are among the many plants from the Arctic, Alps and Mediterranean which grow here on the calcium-rich soil. Maidenhair and hart's tongue fern thrive in the micro-environment of the sheltering grikes. These plants and many others are best seen in the late spring when the flowers are blooming.

2   *Caherdoonfergus*

Caherdoonfergus, or as T. D. Robinson's map sternly puts it, 'Cathair Dhuin Irghuis, miscalled Caherdoonfergus', is a fine example of a large ringfort. This formerly lightly wooded area of well-drained land once attracted a large population, as the many ringforts in the Burren testify. Overgrazing and possibly a climatic change led to erosion and the subsequent uncovering of the bare rock.

3   *The Valley of Gleninagh South*

This area is a fertile contrast to the bare hillside on both sides. The soil is composed of thick glacial deposits which accumulated in the valley. At the end of the walk along the Caher River a cross-section of similar deposits has been exposed by subsidence into the river.

Limestone pavements

115

3·20

THE CENTRAL MAAMTURKS

STARTING AND FINISHING
POINT
The car-park on the north-east
side of the R344 (Lough Inagh
road) 5 miles (8 km) from
Kylemore and $5\frac{1}{2}$ miles (9 km)
from Recess (847533). The car-
park is signposted 'Mamean Tobar
& Leaba Phadraig' in archaic Irish
lettering. If your knowledge of
this lettering is rusty, look for the
sign for Lough Inagh Fishery
directly opposite.
MAPS
The 1:50 000 Connemara map is
recommended. The OS half-inch
to the mile Sheet 10 is on too
small a scale and is recommended
only if nothing else is available.
LENGTH
9 miles (14.5 km)
ASCENT
2750 ft (840 m)

Like other sections of the Maamturks, the rock-ribbed central section, which is the focus of this walk, runs from one high pass to another in a long, gently curving line. Ascending the rock-strewn plateau above, it takes in two major peaks which, depending on the exact point from which they are viewed, rise above the plateau with varying degrees of success. The panorama from the tops, particularly towards the crowded peaks of the Bens, is excellent. The walk reaches the lowlands along a tiny river valley and ends as it began along the Western Way.

ROUTE DESCRIPTION (Map 3.20)

From the car-park leave the R344 to follow the minor road uphill, thus emulating the route of the pilgrims to Mamean (1). Continue along the part-metalled part-pot-holed road (2) passing through the scattered houses at Illion West/An Uillinn Thair after $1\frac{1}{2}$ miles (2.5 km), and at the dip beyond it where stone walls clamber in a higgledy-piggledy way among rising ground on the L look out beyond them and before the river for a place where there is comparatively dry ground on which to start the walk to Mam Ochoige, a high pass in the Maamturks.

Walk upriver towards the pass keeping to the L bank, and pass through the huge, dark rocky ramparts guarding the pass by taking the only significant gap, that taken by the stream. Beyond is level ground, a miniature Shangri La cut off from the world and an ideal spot for rough camping. From here, continue steeply uphill to the pass (3), where the lake shown on the maps is nowhere to be seen. You have not located the wrong gap however. The mystery will soon be revealed.

The route from the pass to the first peak, Knocknahillion/Cnoc na hUilleann (1993 ft/607 m) is a straightforward climb through rough vegetation and scattered boulders. Look back on this ascent to see the sought-for lake lying just above the gap. (If the visibility is good and you *still* don't see, you really have a problem.) This climb also affords good views down into the long, grassy-sided Failmore Valley to the R and behind.

From Knocknahillion the route runs north over a bewildering rocky landscape of tiny hillocks and hidden lochans, narrowing at one point to a narrow but flat neck. Beyond this a bulky cairn beckons — the top of Letterbreckaun/Binn Briocain? Alas, no. It marks the edge of the virtual plateau on which Letterbreckaun (2193 ft/669 m) lies. Having gained this plateau note another cairn, and then another. Exactly which one marks the top is difficult to say with certainty. While this is a good reason to avoid indiscriminate cairning, the cairns are so close together that any confusion should not be too serious.

Map 3.20 : The Central Maamturks

The descent route

Careful navigation is required on the descent over irregular broken ground from Letterbreckaun. To keep on the ridge, head first north-east for a few hundred yards and then north-west for a similar distance. When two tiny lochans are seen, one perched directly above the other, look for a point where a direct descent west into a narrow river valley can be made by taking a gully between crags.

That done, the remainder of the walk is easy. Take either bank downstream (but note that you must end up on the L bank), past a delightful little waterfall. Next note the stone walls and ruin ahead. Keep to their L and cross a fence, an extension L of the wall, at an easy point. Turn half-L to reach the Western Way, at this point a wide track but one which blends chameleon-like into the surrounding bogland, so that an act of faith — and a compass — may be needed to follow it along the foot of the Maamturks close on the L. After $1\frac{1}{4}$ miles (2 km) on the Western Way, forest and a few houses heave into sight. Continue on beyond them, following roughly the electricity poles should the Way be unclear. When the Way reaches a metalled road turn R and walk back to the car-park.

1   *The Pilgrimage to Mamean*
     This pilgrimage takes place in early August each year. The ceremonies connected with it take place at Mamean, a mountain pass 5 miles (8 km) from here. Once a place of pagan worship, it was later Christianized, and later still 'enlivened' by the addition of poteen-drinking and faction-fighting. The pilgrimage was revived recently and now has a more decorous format.

2   *The Western Way*
     At present this Long Distance Route runs from Oughterard in County Galway west and north to Westport in Mayo, taking in some of the most spectacular scenery in the two counties. There are plans to extend it northwards from Westport. The route is not waymarked at present.

The start of the climb

3   The Maamturks Walk

This marathon walk, which takes place in May each year, is reputed to be the toughest in Ireland. It passes south-east to north-west by Mam Ochoige. Fifteen miles (24 km) long with a climb of 8000 ft (2430 m), it takes in the entire length of the Maamturks from the Maam Cross-Maam Bridge road to Leenane. The descents and re-ascents from the five major passes, of which Mam Ochoige is one, make it particularly arduous. The record for the walk is about 5 hours, nearly half Naismith Rule's reckoning and this does not allow any time for stops.

3·21

MWEELREA

On the R335/L100 (Glenanane to
Louisburgh road) just north of
Doo Lough (830694), where
there is ample parking on the
roadside. From Leenane turn L off
the N59 or from Westport turn R
off the N59 onto the R335, and
park 8 miles (13 km) beyond this
turn at the far end of Doo Lough.
MAPS
OS half-inch to the mile Sheet 10
covers the area — after a fashion.
See the safety note below.
LENGTH
10 miles (16 km)
ASCENT
3400 ft (1030 m)
SAFETY NOTE
Mweelrea is not a mountain to be
trifled with, and the only map
available is unreliable and on far
too small a scale for detailed
navigation. Therefore, think
carefully before attempting the
climb on a bad day. Under all
conditions leave yourself plenty of
time. Two routes are described to
the massif. If you suffer from
vertigo or wish to avoid some airy
scrambling, take the easier one.

At 2686 ft (819 m) Mweelrea (pronounced '*Mweel-ray*') is the
highest peak in the West. Perhaps peak is not quite the right
word: Mweelrea is, rather, the highest point of a massif, an
undulating grassy area whose eastern side is abruptly terminated
by a gigantic and magnificent corrie — one of several which has
eaten into the massif. It is along the corrie edge that the other
high points of the massif rise, 'half-peaks' with innocent grassy
slopes on one side and the wicked plunging wall of the corrie on
the other. The route's focal point is this corrie, but it also pays its
respects to Mweelrea itself on the far end of the plateau, from
which the views are stunning.

ROUTE DESCRIPTION (Map 3.21)

If there is good visibility it might be helpful to study the route
before starting — most of it can be seen from the road. The
difficult route climbs directly up the northern (R) arm of the huge
corrie on the opposite side of Doo Lough, ascends a small subsidiary peak, from your standpoint well below the skyline, and then
advances directly up to the summit plateau. The *easy* route
climbs the back wall of the corrie on a grassy ramp rising L to R to
a low point on the summit plateau. Here the routes converge for
the final ascent.

The difficult route Cross the stream flowing into Doo Lough
using stepping-stones near the lough, cross the fence beyond and
advance across the bog where, in dry weather, sundews *(1)* are
particularly evident. As you climb along the inner side of the
arm, watch out for a solitary rowan tree and take a narrow gully
20 yards (18 m) or so to its R. If this causes vertigo, retreat
forthwith to the easy variation. A little further up, the summit
plateau appears — bands of gently dipping sandstone strata with
no evident way of breaching the ramparts they form.

Undeterred, climb the small peak mentioned above, and head
for the rocky nose beyond, where the crux of the route awaits.
Keep first to the L of the nose along a faint but reassuring path,
scramble up the airy staircase, and then make a frontal scramble
through rocks which ends in an easily climbed arête. Above this
is the grass of the summit plateau.

STARTING AND FINISHING POINT

Louisburgh

Glencullin L.

small subsidiary peak

R335

Doo Lough

① Hard route

Benbury

Easy route

③

② Mweelrea △
.750

L.Bellawaum

Ben Lugmore
600

600

450

450

Lugaloughan L.

300

300

Ruin

150

Owennaglogh River

Fin Lough

KILLARY HARBOUR

R335

Bundorragha R.

300

Leenane

Map 3.21 : Mweelrea

| 0 | | 1 | | 2 | | 3 Kilometres |
| 0 | | | 1 | | | 2 Miles |

The easy route Follow the difficult route to the sundews. Then follow the stream that runs into the north-west corner of Doo Lough. This leads into a valley where you can find your way over, or circumvent, low cliffs. Above the cliffs, ascend the grassy ramp and at its top climb an easy gully L to the lowest point in the corrie rim. Turn R (north-east) to reach the grassy plateau. Here the two routes converge.

From the plateau, walk to Benbury (2610 ft/796 m), which rises none too ostentatiously a few hundred yards further to the north-west, after which head to Mweelrea (2686 ft/819 m) over catastrophically sparse grass *(2)*. The summit area of Mweelrea is undistinguished, but as a viewpoint it is unsurpassed. Killary Harbour winds its sinuous way close at hand, beyond which crowd the Benchoonas, the Twelve Bens and the Maamturks. The Sheffry Hills and Ben Gorm rise to the east. Northwards is

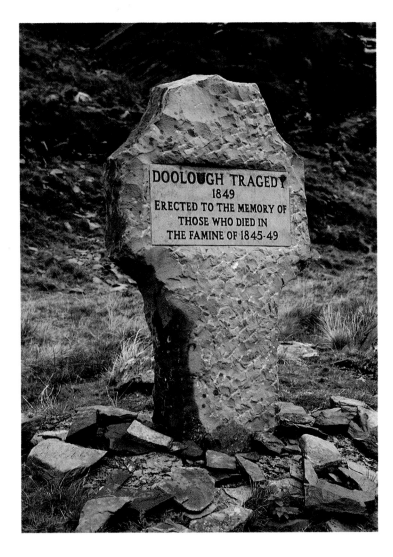

The Doo Lough Tragedy memorial

bog and fringing the sea the magnificent beach at Killadoon runs far northwards. Beyond it to the west a scattering of islands ride the ocean.

Return along the ascent route, bypassing Benbury, to reach the main corrie edge at its lowest point once more. A dramatic jagged skyline lies ahead. Note here, to the L of the giant 'tooth' rearing skyward, the flat-topped peak Ben Lugmore (2616 ft/797 m). Following the route from this point is child's play. Keep the corrie's rim on the L on a roller-coaster progress, veering R onto grassy slopes where rock formations bar the way.

At Ben Lugmore, take care not to follow the grassy spur south-east; instead swing L to keep close to the corrie rim, here not quite so impressive. Continue steeply downhill, forking L over rocky ground onto the higher branch where the spur divides.

The steep and punishing descent resumes after the rocky ground. As you near the road (it is of course the R335 again) watch out for a ruin between it and the Bundorragha River. Ford the river here (alas, wet feet may be unavoidable) to gain the road, turn L and walk back to the starting point. On this walk, a pleasant one offering varying angles on the day's route, look out on the R for the plaque to the victims of the Doo Lough tragedy in 1849 *(3)*.

1   *The Sundew*
    The sundew is a typical plant of the bogs and is easily recognizable because of the bright red splashes that its leaves impart to the otherwise dull-coloured stretches of bog. It makes up for the lack of minerals in its environment by the simple process of catching mineral-rich insects. This it does by trapping unlucky insects on its sticky tentacles and then dissolving and absorbing them.

2   *Erosion on the Hilltops*
    This area has suffered greatly from over-grazing by sheep, caused by the EC Common Agricultural Policy which gives grants on the basis of the number of ewes run by each farmer, so that it is in each farmer's interest to run the maximum. The result is the erosion evident here (see p. 17).

3   *Tragedy at Doo Lough*
    In 1849, towards the end of the Great Famine, a comparatively small and little-known, yet significant tragedy occurred hereabouts. A group of starving people who were trying to seek refuge in the workhouse at Louisburgh were advised to present themselves in person to the Guardians of the Workhouse at Delphi, 12 miles (19 km) away over rough tracks. The Guardians could — or would — do nothing for them, so the starving people had to return through the cold of an early spring. Some of them died on the way back. While the numbers involved are disputed, the main facts and therefore the poignancy of the incident is not. This event is remembered in a simple plaque on the side of the road here.

Mweelrea: the eastern side

THE GLENCOAGHAN HORSESHOE

STARTING AND FINISHING POINT

Ben Lettery Youth Hostel (777483) on the N59, 6 miles (9.5 km) west of Recess and 8 miles (13 km) east of Clifden. The Hostel is on the northern side of the road and is well signposted. There is plenty of space for safe parking. Two miles (3 km) of tedious walking can be avoided if two cars are used, the second leaving the walkers about 1 mile (1.6 km) along the track described in the first paragraph of the route description. Here there is room for careful parking on the verge.

MAPS

The 1:50 000 Connemara map is recommended. The OS half-inch to the mile Sheet 10 is on too small a scale and should be used only if nothing else is available.

LENGTH

10 miles (16 km)

ASCENT

5200 feet (1590 m)

SAFETY NOTE

Although the total distance walked is modest, there is a lot of climbing and the descents can be just as tiring as the ascents. Be prepared for a long, energetic day.

This is a classic among Irish hill walks, a demanding circuit taking in six of the rearing Twelve Bens in a lofty route over steeply rising and dipping terrain. It is the bare quartzite rock that distinguishes the walk from nearly all others in Ireland, and which gives it its unique character. The views all along the route are excellent: primarily the ever-changing vista of the Bens themselves into whose deepest recesses this walk penetrates. But that is not all: the Maamturks lie just across the Inagh Valley, and between Bens and Maamturks and curving round in a great arc to the south (thus blocking off the Bens from the watery bogland further south) runs a long, narrow scenic line of interconnected lakes. A superb walk in superb country.

ROUTE DESCRIPTION (Map 4.22)

With the Hostel on the L walk along the N59 for 1 mile (1.6 km), turning first L here onto a track. This track must constitute one of the most untidy and unprepossessing starts of any walk: 'temporary' caravan dwellings, straggling fences and rough ground combine to deter the sensitive walker. But persevere; after about 1 mile (1.6 km) of undulating progress, the full view of the circuit broken only by the curious snout pushing east of Benbreen/Binn Bhraoin comes fully into view. It is a magnificent sweep of peaks from Derryclare/Binn Dhoir Chlair nearby on the R to Ben Lettery/Binn Leitri on the L, vegetation climbing the lower slopes, glistening quartzite above to the very summits.

Choose any convenient point along here to leave the track and head half R for Derryclare (2220 ft/677 m) which rises steeply close at hand. Initially, the ground is rough and boggy, but it improves if a grassy ramp higher up, not essential for route-finding, is found. There is a long, unrelenting climb to the summit of Derryclare, which marks the end of vegetation; from here on, the route is predominantly over rock all the way to Ben Lettery. A short drop and rather longer rise *(1)* ends in Bencorr/Binn Chorr (2336 ft/712 m) where the views to Lough Inagh, and beyond that to the Maamturks, catch the eye.

Take the ridge of rock slabs heading initially north-west from Bencorr and drop to the pass at Mam na bhFonsai, taking care not to follow the formidable range running north-east that ends overlooking Lough Inagh. From the pass, climb sharply to Bencollaghduff/Binn Dhubh (2260 ft/698 m), a magnificent belvedere in the centre of the Bens, and commanding especially good views of the white cone of Benbaun/Binn Bhan, at 2395 ft (730 m) the highest of all the Bens.

Map 4.22 : The Glencoaghan Horseshoe

Another steep drop, partly over narrow but safe ground, follows to Maumina/Mam Eidheach, a narrow, comparatively low pass (1476 ft/450 m), which is generally considered to be the centre around which the peaks of the Bens converge *(2)*. Three valleys meet, or rather nearly meet here: the partly wooded valley of the Owenglin river running west, the unwooded part of which is in the Connemara National Park *(3)*; Glencoaghan to the south; and Gleninagh/Gleann Eidhneach, not visible from here but only a little way off to the north-east. Between these three the highest pyramids of the Bens soar skywards, bare and awe-inspiring. Would it be an earthward descent into bathos to mention also that Maumina is an excellent place for a rest and a snack?

There is another steep climb with some avoidable scrambling to Benbreen/Binn Bhraoin (2276 ft/694 m), a difficult peak on which to navigate in bad weather. The initial climb ends in a rock-strewn plateau and a dog-leg L on it brings you to the summit cairn on the far end. If in doubt note that the eastern spur of Benbreen which projects unmistakably into the main valley is directly opposite the summit.

A steep scree descent, partly (but only partly) avoidable ends at another narrow pass. From here Bengower/Binn Gabhar (2184 ft/666 m) is due south. Once again and unsurprisingly, another steep ascent to the summit (you will surely be used to them by now!), this one involving some scrambling, though this is neither difficult nor vertigo-inducing.

South of Bengower, grass once again begins to predominate. Ben Lettery (1904 ft/580 m) *(4)* is but a short stroll away, but take care on this stretch *not* to follow the spur R towards Benglenisky/Binn Ghleann Uisce. Descend south of Ben Lettery towards the Hostel and the road through steep, rough wet vegetation. As you descend, the Hostel, partly obscured by clumps of trees,comes into view, and as is usual on difficult, lengthy descents at the end of a tiring day, seems to get no whit more prominent as you walk.

At length you will see a ruin ahead. Head for this, crossing the fence just before it (look for the place where the wires are bent to facilitate walkers). Cross the track ahead and near the Hostel go to the R side to use the stile at the boundary fence. Take the driveway to the road.

1   The Patient Surveyor
The remains of a stone shelter just above the col towards Bencorr was occupied by an OS surveyor in the 1840s when the major triangulation of Ireland was being carried out. He had to wait 7 weeks to get a clear day to see what he called the 'Kerry Man' on Carrauntoohil 90 miles (145 km) away.

Opposite: The eastern end of the Bens

2 *Muckanaght, the Green Hill*

From Maumina the peak of Muckanaght/Meacanach to the north-west may be seen. It is more rounded and greener than its neighbours, the reason being that alone among the Bens it is formed of schists, not quartzite. The schist breaks down easier than the quartzite, thus giving a gentler outline and forming better soil, which allows some grass to cling to its sides.

3 *The Connemara National Park*

The Connemara National Park takes in the near sides (only) of the three summits north and west of here as well as the summit of Bencullagh/An Chailleach and the area around it to the west. The Park stretches to the outskirts of Letterfrack, $5\frac{1}{2}$ miles (9 km) away. In all it covers 5000 acres (2000 hectares), mostly mountain but also with some areas of bog, heaths and grassland. The Visitor Centre at Letterfrack, which is open from Easter to the end of September, provides an audio-visual display, a stunning photographic display of Connemara scenery (though not as stunning as the display you should be experiencing here at Maumina), and picnic tables with the free use of electric kettles to brew your own hot drinks (the latter are not free). The Visitor Centre is a good excursion for a wet day.

4 *Caesar Otway on Ben Lettery*

Mr Caesar Otway, whom we last met on Muckish, also climbed Ben Lettery, which he found 'extremely rugged and precipitous'. He had a different type of anguish on Lettery to that which he experienced on Muckish. 'Some of our party', he thundered, 'called for the provision basket. It was little short of treason against the majesty of nature, to fix those eyes on rolls and cold beef, which ought to have been directed to one of the noblest views of Cunnemarra.'

It is more than likely that eating and viewing simultaneously would have compounded the affront.

The view across Glencoaghan

INTRODUCTION

The mountains of the South-West, in effect the mountains of County Kerry since the contiguous hill area of west Cork is but a small adjunct, boast nearly all the highest mountains in Ireland, including all but two of its Munros. This paramount but simple fact does not itself make the mountains of Kerry attractive or challenging, but nevertheless they are. Tall (as small) *is* beautiful.

This is an area where the sea, and its numerous inlets, are never far away. The mountains are located on five peninsulas, five rugged fingers reaching westward into the ocean and separated by long, tapering bays — in geological terms drowned valleys. In many mountain areas the sea is ever-present, a deep blue plain stretching to the misty horizon. In others it reveals itself on the climb: sections of what appear first as disjointed lakes coalesce with height to be seen eventually as long inlets of the sea.

The other common feature of the South-West is the relative abundance of vegetation. The area benefits from the warmth of the Gulf Stream and so is characterized by exceptionally mild winters, especially in its southernmost reaches. In particular the area round Glengarriff in the far south is a humid hothouse of vegetation, so that the frequent epithet 'sub-tropical' that is applied to the region is not altogether an exaggeration.

The long inlets and rugged terrain mean that access is not easy in the South-West. Roads hug the coast and cross the peninsulas only by means of tortuous, sinuous passes. Add to that the perennial poor state of the roads so that the rule must be: leave yourself plenty of time for travel; you will probably need it.

In an area of splendid mountains some of the routes were 'musts'. The Coomloughra horseshoe simply had to be included. How could any mountaineering writer omit a circuit which encompasses the *three* highest peaks in Ireland and by far its most spectacular ridge walk? Brandon was in the same category: a great massif on the Dingle Peninsula, a superb juxtaposition of magnificent corrie, rugged hillside and rolling ocean — and a formidable Monro to boot.

Some of the others were not so obvious; two at least were chosen because they are characteristic of their areas. The proud peak of Mullaghanattin is near the centre of Iveragh, the largest by far of the five peninsulas, and provides one fine circuit among

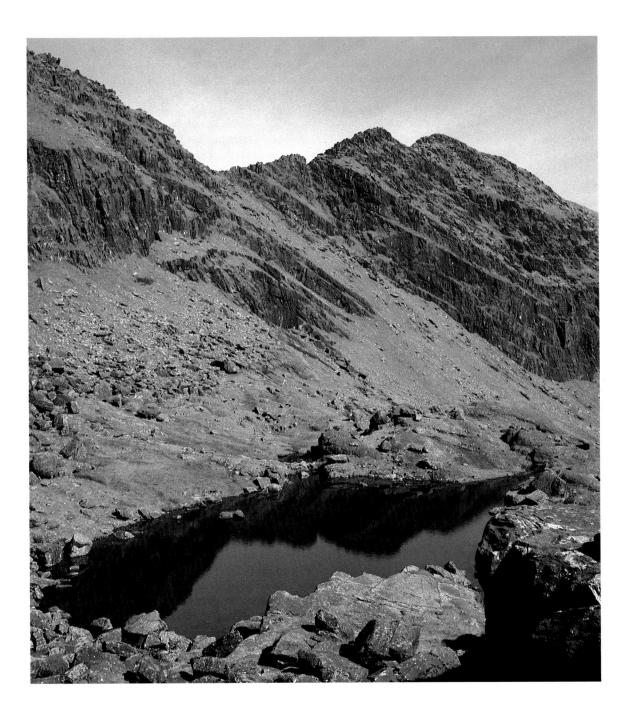

A Paternoster lake on Brandon

many in an area of great mountain country. Several other routes almost as attractive might have been chosen instead of (or preferably in addition to) Mullaghanattin. Further south the Beara Peninsula presented a similarly difficult choice. An area of lush vegetation, highly characteristic sandstone rock formations, but dull uplands, it was no easy matter to pick the best route. Nonetheless the Cummeengeera horseshoe is difficult to better.

The two routes which are easily accessible from Killarney are close only in their location. Bennaunmore is a purely serendipitous discovery: on the map an unpromising hilly area first chosen to while away a day of low cloud. However, a pleasant surprise was in store: regions far greater in extent and several times as high cannot boast a terrain as varied and as mountainously rugged, where each few steps reveal fresh delights. The other area near Killarney is quite different, partly open moorland offering wide views, the haunt of the endangered red deer, partly (if you choose the route variation) dramatic rocky defile. This is one of the few routes in comparatively pathless Ireland where a satisfactory circuit can be made purely on path and track. Incidentally, do not be put off by the length of this route. The text also describes shorter alternatives.

The other two routes have connotations other than purely mountaineering ones. Mount Eagle is as much a cultural as a physical journey. At the remote end of the remote Dingle Peninsula it gives not only a highly scenic coastal walk, but also a glimpse into the remnants of Gaelic Ireland, the archaeological and linguistic remains of a once-rich culture now on a life-support system. Lastly, Gougane Barra, which has religious associations as well as cultural ones, is undoubtedly the finest area for walking in West Cork, both because of the dramatic views it gives of the corrie on which the route centres and the wide panorama it allows.

2·23

Mount Eagle

STARTING AND FINISHING
POINT
In the car-park on the seaward
side of the R559 just south of the
village of Coumeenoole (317976).
MAP
OS half-inch to the mile Sheet 20
is barely adequate. (OS 1:50 000
Sheet 70 is scheduled for 1991).
LENGTH
7 miles (10 km)
ASCENT
1700 ft (530 m)

For much of this walk the eye is drawn irresistibly towards the sea, and especially towards the islands which lie scattered over it. Pre-eminent is Great Blasket, a basking whale of a rock just off the pointing finger of Dunmore Head. Beyond it float the other islands of the Blaskets: Inishtooskert, Tearaght, Inishnabro and Inishvickillane — all of them carrying almost mystic significance for the last phase of Gaelic-speaking Ireland. Further away to the south rise the unmistakable Great and Little Skelligs, like the summits of jagged peaks rising sheer out of the ocean. Add to all this splendid views of the mountains of two peninsulas and the result is an easy yet rewarding walk of excellent and varied views.

ROUTE DESCRIPTION (Map 2.23)

With the car-park on the R walk 300 yards (270 m) south along the road and turn L at the 'walking-man' sign to go through a gate. Turn R immediately and follow the wall in which the gate is set, first parallel to the main road and then steeply uphill. Pass another 'walking-man' on your L *(1), (2)*, still following the wall. Where the wall turns sharply R continue straight ahead uphill along an intermittent wall and earth bank which constitutes a boundary line.

This boundary line can be easily followed all the way to the top of Mount Eagle: first fairly steeply uphill, then over rocks and steep ground at Beenacouma (1395 ft/425 m), where it almost disappears, and finally over grass on the nearly level stretch near the summit (1696 ft, 517 m), which is marked by an OS obelisk.

From the summit, head towards the corrie that holds Mt Eagle Lough to pick up the end of a green track. Walk north along it, with the cliff and lough to the R, continuing straight ahead where a branch on the R heads down the northern side of the corrie.

Follow the track all the way to the Dunquin–Kildurrihy road, turn R here and again L at the T-junction, which has three signposts, all pointing to Daingean (Gaelic for Dingle). And you thought all roads led to Rome! Keep on this road, crossing the base of Dunmore Head *(3)*, to reach the car-park.

Map 2.23: Mount Eagle

Dunmore Head

STARTING AND
FINISHING POINT

Coumeenoole

'Walking
man'
signs

① ② ③

Mt Eagle
Lake

Mt. Eagle ▲

450

△ Beenacouma

300

150

150

300

0   1   2   3 Kilometres

0   1   2 Miles

Left: *Slea Head from Ventry*

Below: *A shrine on the Slea Head road*

1   *The Slea Head Road*

The road on which this walk starts was built in the second half of the nineteenth century to relieve unemployment. This type of civil work, some of it of negligible practical use, was the usual palliative to relieve a problem which has never been satisfactorily solved except by the expedient of emigration.

2   *The Blaskets*

The Great Blasket Island was inhabited until 1953, wholly by Gaelic speakers. In that year the remaining inhabitants were evacuated. There was a fine tradition of writing among the islanders, the best known of whom, Peig Sayers, is buried in the graveyard close to the end of the walk.

The best map of the Blaskets is popular everywhere in Ireland, among cartographers and non-cartographers alike. Only a few inches long and not a rarity, it is nonetheless quite valuable. It is universally known — and valued — as the Irish £20 note.

3   *Aftermath of the Armada*

A Spanish ship foundered in Blasket Sound between Dunmore Head and Great Blasket in September 1588 after the disastrous rout of the Armada. Hundreds of Spanish were drowned and only one, the pilot's son, was saved and he was captured. A Spanish prince who was among those lost is buried in the old burial ground at Dunquin.

2·24

GOUGANE BARRA

Opposite the church at Gougane
Barra (091657), where there is
ample parking. Gougane Barra is
off the R584/T64 (Macroom–
Ballylickey road) on the R
travelling from Macroom.
It is well signposted.

MAPS

OS half-inch to the mile Sheet 24
inadequately covers the route.
Sheet 21 covers the area just
north of the route and is useful
for identifying features beyond
Sheet 24.

LENGTH

7 miles (11 km)

ASCENT

1750 ft (530 m)

SAFETY NOTE

This is a moderately short walk
with what should be a simple
navigational objective: to keep the
corrie on the R. However, there
are few significant landmarks —
the 'peaks' barely rise above the
plateau so in bad visibility you
should use the small landmarks,
primarily the lochans, to
determine your position. There
are only a few places where a
direct descent to the valley floor
can be attempted.

Gougane Barra (pronounced *Goo-gawn Barra*) is the jewel in the
crown of the Shehy mountains of West Cork. The curious name
properly refers to the narrow lake whose only major island contains a tiny picturesque church surrounded by trees. West of the
lake a long, partly wooded corrie indented by several side valleys
is cut into the plateau of the Shehy mountains. The walk circum-
scribes this corrie in a wide, clockwise sweep. With no real
summits to be climbed, the walk's interest centres on the views
of the lake and corrie, but more so outwards to the Paps, the
great corrie of Lough Nambrackderg and the further-off jagged
outline of the Reeks.

ROUTE DESCRIPTION (Map 2.24)

With the car-park on the L *(1)* walk along the road for 80 yards
(70 m), turning L here through a gate and up a minor track at a
toilet disguised as a circular African straw-hut. Follow the track
uphill until it resolutely heads south-east, clearly the wrong
direction. Strike diagonally R uphill here, cross a fence, and then
aim for a rocky pinnacle high above. Not a peak, this is nonetheless a clear landmark. Its name, Foilastookeen, means 'The cliff
of the little pinnacle' and this is a good description.

From here the next target is the unnamed peak close by to the
south-west where a fence is visible on the skyline. Around this
peak the views open up outwards from Gougane Barra corrie;
Bantry Bay and the aptly named voluptuous Paps being conspicuous. Keeping the fence on the L follow it over rough ground past
three small lakes on the L. At the last of these lakes (where the
fence ends) a grid bearing of 350° will be needed to find Lough
Glas high on the plateau to the north-west.

From Lough Glas continue slightly downwards to the head of a
gully R *(2)*, crossing a fence close to it to reach a lochan. At this
point the immense corrie of Lough Nambrackderg with a long,
narrow waterfall plunging into it, can be seen at its finest. Continue across wet bogland to Bealick (1764 ft/538 m), the only
'peak' (a courtesy title) on this route to have a cairn of any sort.
Given the number of hillocks hereabouts it is a useful construction.

The walk would appear to be almost over, with only a descent R to the start. Not so. The cliffs overlooking Gougane Barra Lake are low but dangerous, and though they can be circumvented the safe routes are easier to find in retrospect. Keep therefore to the shoulder north-east from Bealick, walking to a small lake set in quaking bog and continue straight ahead beyond it, dropping off the L side of the nose facing the Owenashrone River. Turn R at the river and follow the L bank down through tussocky country to a small copse of conifers where the river swings R. Cross wet bogland here to a narrow metalled road *(3)*, turn R along it and L at the foot of the hill (R leads to the nearby substantial farm-house). At the main road turn R for the starting point.

1   The Church at Gougane Barra
The small church on Holy Island opposite the car-park, which can be reached by a causeway, dates from as recently as 1900 and was inspired by a chapel on the Rock of Cashel. The stone court nearby dates from the end of the seventeenth century. The wooden cross in the centre of the court is

Map 2.24 :
Gougane Barra

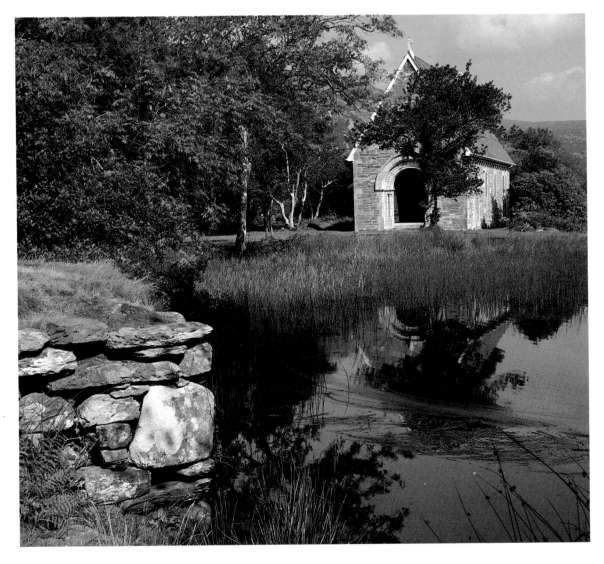

The Church at Gougane Barra

inscribed in Latin, English and Gaelic: 'here stood in the sixth century, the cell of St Finbar, first bishop of Cork'. St Finbar had a monastery here which, being constructed of simple perishable material, has long since disappeared.

2   *The Fortuitous Gully*

This gully played a happy role for Irish insurgents in May 1921 when rebel troops were hemmed in on all sides by superior British forces. Helped by local guides the rebels retreated into Gougane Barra, and at night, led by a local guide, they climbed a long rope up this gully and thus escaped into Kerry.

3   *The Pilgrim's Road*

This road marks the end of the pilgrims' route into Gougane Barra, the start of which is noted in Route 25.

Opposite: *Gougane Barra lake*

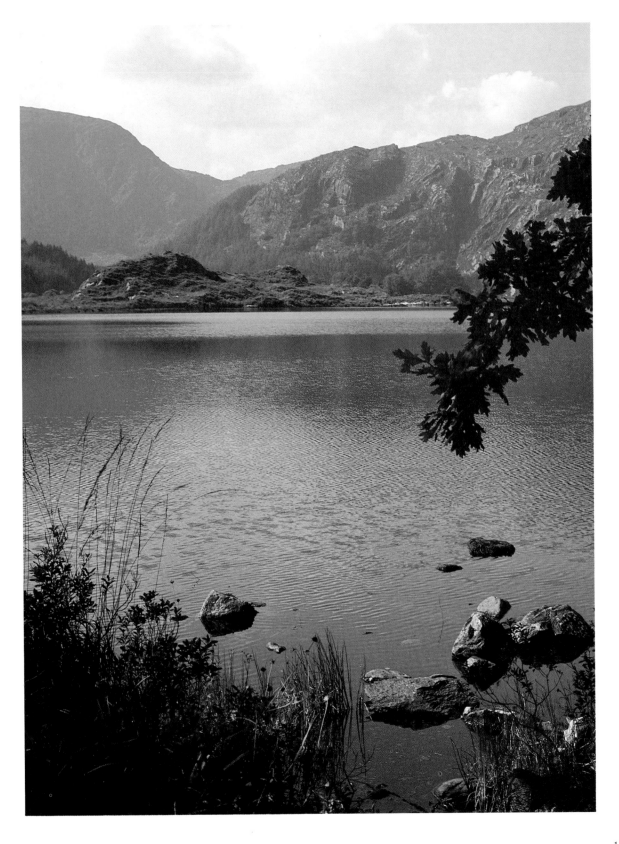

2·25

BENNAUNMORE

STARTING AND FINISHING
POINT

At the end of the side-road
running along the eastern side of
the Lough Guitane (034839).
From Killarney take the N71
(Kenmare road) turning L at the
signpost 'Lough Guitane $2\frac{1}{2}$',
which is just after the jarveys'
gathering-point about $2\frac{1}{2}$ miles
(4 km) from Killarney. Drive
straight ahead for 4 miles
(6.4 km), turning R onto a gated
road here. Drive for a further 1.4
miles (2.2 km) and park on open
ground near a bridge which serves
a farmhouse.

MAPS

OS half-inch to the mile Sheet 21
covers the route, though very
inadequately. Sheet 20 in the
same series also covers the route
unless you intend to get lost
eastwards! (The route is at the
very edge of this map.) (OS
1:50 000 Sheet 79 is scheduled
for end 1991.)

LENGTH

$6\frac{1}{2}$ miles (10.5 km)

ASCENT

1650 ft (500 m)

The area south-east of Killarney close to Lough Guitane is ideal
for leisurely free-range exploration. The discriminating walker
can enjoy narrow but deep glens, low but soaring peaks flanked
by impressive cliffs, ancient oakwoods and tiny hidden lakes, all
in a virtually unfrequented area within a couple of miles of Bennaunmore, a peak of volcanic rock. The route given here is a
suggestion only, a vehicle to point to the small-scale hidden
delights of the area. Take into account the few cautions given
below and you can wander around safely as the fancy takes you.
Give yourself plenty of time: much of the terrain is difficult —
and all of it repays leisurely pottering.

ROUTE DESCRIPTION (Map 2.25)

Follow the track south-east (that is, not over the bridge) past a
ruin on the L. Cross two minor streams, and just beyond the
second pass through a gate. This gate marks your entry into open
country and you should note carefully its position since you will
have to find it on the return.

From the gate head south-east (exactly 120° grid) towards a
tiny valley visible from here. Walk up the valley (1). ('Walk' is a
euphemism for struggle: crossing from one bank to the other and
back again, clambering over rocks, climbing through high vegetation, and even stone-hopping up the stream when all else
fails.) After at least a half-hour's work with little progress to
show for it, you will gain a tiny basin with a hill beyond flanked
by two valleys, that to the R sheltering a small copse of oaks.
Follow this valley, which gives unexpectedly easy going over
long grass, up to a grassy col. Lough Nabroda comes suddenly
into view below, and the rocky cliffs on the eastern flank of
Bennaunmore (2) come equally suddenly into view ahead. A good
spot to rest after your strenuous efforts.

Walk down to the near side of the lake to pick up a path
running beside it on its L-hand side. Follow the path to the end of
the lake, where it disappears, leaving the walker to face the wet
grassy bogland beyond to Lake Crohane alone. Here you have
a choice: a difficult route through a mixed wood on the west
(i.e. R) side or an easy route through grass and heather on the

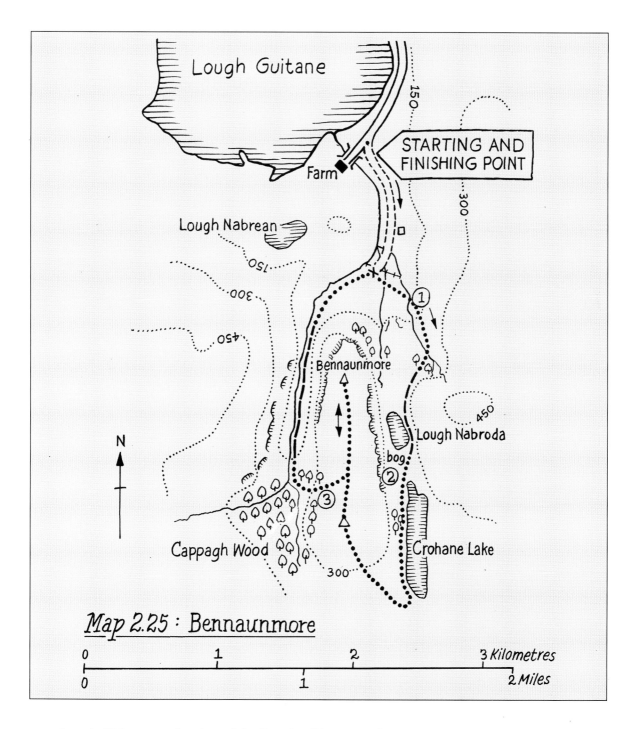

Map 2.25 : Bennaunmore

east (i.e. L). Either way, the view of the Roughty River over the
brow of the hill at the southern end is worth a peep.

Next, Bennaunmore (1490 ft/454 m). The south top is easily
climbed directly from the far south end of Lake Crohane over
rough open country. The north top is a there-and-back to the
saddle between it and the south top, but is worth the effort for

Bennaunmore from near the start

the views it gives of Lough Guitane and the high plateau of Mangerton to the west. At the saddle once again descend carefully west into Cappagh Glen *(3)*. This is a steep slope through an ancient 'petrified' wood of oak, holly and birch whose recumbent branches are not for grasping trustingly — they are all too liable to break off in rotten fragments in the hand. Incidentally, the descent directly from Lake Crohane into the south of Cappagh Glen is not recommended: this slope is even more hazardous than the one described.

On the valley floor turn R (north) to walk by a stream on its R-hand bank. This leads to an impressive natural amphitheatre a little way on, the walls especially high on Bennaunmore's flank to the R and a clear indication that a descent anywhere from Bennaunmore's west flank would be suicidal. At this point the amphitheatre looks exitless: luckily the stream has found a narrow but easy passage, so simply follow it along a clear path.

Beyond the exit follow the burgeoning stream into an alluvial plain of short grass and after a distinct bend to the R veer away from it to gain the gate crossed earlier in the day (the fence ahead will halt onward progress anyway). Take the track beyond, the initial track of the day, directly to the car.

1   *The Old Pilgrim Road*
The stone uprights occasionally seen along here are the remains of an old pilgrim road which led from the plains of Kerry north of here across the mountains to Gougane Barra in west Cork. The pilgrims gathered there for the festival of St Finbar on the last Sunday in September. We have already met the other end of this route in Route 24.

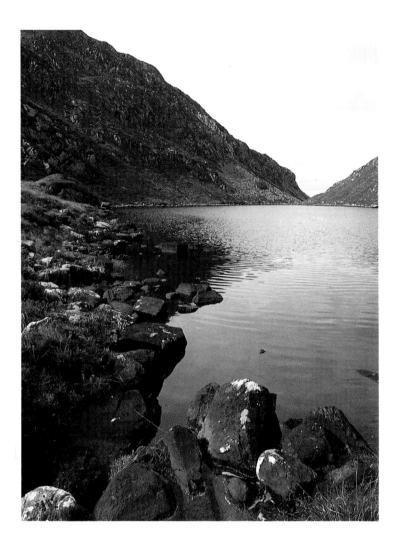

Lough Nabroda

2   *The Giant's Causeway of Kerry*
     The volcanic columnar cliffs of Bennaunmore range for about
     a $\frac{1}{4}$ mile (0.4 km) and in places are about 200 ft (60 m) high.
     Only some of the columns exhibit a regular polygonal cross-
     section. They are not safe for climbing as they come away
     easily from the cliff face. There is a stream flowing north
     from Lough Nabroda but it is underground, being blocked by
     fallen columns and scree from Bennaunmore.

3   *The Petrified Forest of Cappagh*
     This forest, because of its remote location and difficult
     underfoot terrain survived the mass clearing of the native oak
     to make charcoal for iron-smelting furnaces in the seven-
     teenth century. Many of the trees to the south are leafless,
     hence the term 'petrified'. 'Cappagh' (ceapach) is the Gaelic
     for 'decayed', indicating that the forest must have been in
     decline for many years.

THE CUMMEENGEERA HORSESHOE

STARTING AND FINISHING
POINT
On the road into Cummeengeera
(760559). Drive to Lauragh
village, a strung-out few houses,
church, school and post office
around the junction of the
R571/L62 with the R574 (the
Healy Pass road). Taking the
initial measurement from this
crossroads, drive west, that is,
towards Castletown Berehaven,
for 0.8 miles (1.3 km). Turn L
here, signposted 'Glanmore
Lake'. Turn R after 0.6 miles
(1.0 km) and drive for nearly 1
mile (1.4 km) to a gated track on
the R beyond which is a
bungalow. There is limited
parking here or towards the L
turn a few hundred yards further
on.
MAP
OS Kerry District one-inch to the
mile map.
LENGTH
6½ miles (10.5 km)
ASCENT
2450 ft (750 m)

'Benches' are a notable feature of this walk in the Beara Peninsula. The word 'benches' conjures up a smooth horizontal surface, but used by the locals this is a gross misnomer: the great sandstone slabs called 'benches' lie tilted at high, awkward angles and rise line upon line to form the hills, so that on the skyline they appear like the teeth of a huge circular saw. Along their grain walking is easy; a route crossing them is painfully slow.

The other remarkable feature of this area is the luxuriant vegetation in the lowlands: oakwoods drape themselves over the lower slopes and crowd around lakes; rhododendrons, ferns, mosses and a hundred species of flora thrive in the mild climate and high humidity. All quite memorable when viewed from above, but tortuous when traversed lower down.

ROUTE DESCRIPTION (Map 2.26)

Take the track on the R of the road through two gates, turning L off it before the first farmhouse. A tough climb *(1)*, initially through bracken though along the grain of the benches, ensues to the top of Cumeennahillan (1183 ft/361 m), or rather the tops (there are several), one of which is graced by a few heaped stones masquerading as a cairn.

A short drop through wet, boggy country ends in a climb with the grain of the benches to Knocknaveachal (1685 ft/514 m) which has no cairn, but a jagged pinnacle acts as a satisfactory substitute. From here the convoluted folding of Tooth Mountain ahead can be seen to perfection, one fold uncannily like the imprint of the lower set of a giant's teeth *(2)*.

A distinct, avoidable vertical slab is a reassuring landmark on the route to Tooth Mountain (1945 ft/593 m), the climb to which is short but difficult, through high slabs and along grassy ledges. The top is a tangle of rocky outcrops and puddles with no clear landmark to indicate position.

The terrain changes markedly after Tooth Mountain, slabs yielding to grassy bogland, thus allowing speedier progress. Coomacloghane (1969 ft/600 m) is another indefinite top or rather would be were it not for its OS obelisk. After Coomacloghane, slabs re-appear intermittently as far as the peat-hagged plateau that lies along the Cork-Kerry border. Once on this plateau, swing L to keep to the edge of the steep ground at the head of Cummeengeera. Along here the great rocky bulk of Hungry Hill to the south-east dominates the skyline.

Walk along level ground to Eskatarriff (1973 ft/601 m), an unimpressive set of slabs, after which climb a small but steep pinnacle, unheralded on the maps. This is Bireca, its L flank dropping sheer into the inner recesses of Cummeengeera. The upper end of the valley visible from here is interesting. Separated

Map 2.26 : Cummeengeera Horseshoe

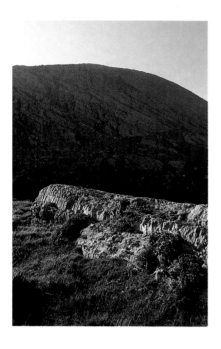

A 'bench' below Tooth mountain

from the lower end of Cummeengeera by a steep climb along a track, the valley is now deserted though it retains the traces of field boundaries and the remains of a house *(3)*, all of which from this lofty viewpoint appear as though on a map.

The next target is Lackbane (1984 ft/604 m), a stiff climb through rocky terrain. Beyond this, climb Curraghreague (1970 ft/600 m), its sister peak, which has a small cairn and whose north-west side drops far down into the glen in rock formations which look like organ pipes.

From Curraghreague make a steep descent over narrow ground offering excellent views of Lake Glanmore to the R and the lovely wooded lake and inlet country ahead. The drop ends at a narrow pass where the tempting direct descent L should not be attempted; it contains a wicked terrain of bracken and hidden boulder. Instead climb the hill directly ahead (it is only 100 ft/ 30 m or so) and descend north heading for the grassy circular mound below *(4)*. Take the path to its L, cross the area where it appears as if rhododendrons have been deliberately planted (surely not!) and carry on north to pick up a track.

Follow this across a bridge of rock slabs and through a gate. Beyond this turn L onto a better track at a hairpin bend (on the better track). Follow this track over a bridge to a metalled road and turn R for the starting point.

1 *Sub-tropical Gardens at Dereen*
The woods of the Dereen Tropical Gardens just beyond Lauragh should be visible on the ascent. Built up over 130 years, the gardens flourish in the warm, damp climate. They include New Zealand ferns which although rare in the British Isles, thrive here; and giant conifers of north-west America, some of which are over 100 ft (30 m) tall.

2 *A Dental Mix-up at the Ordnance Survey*
Knocknaveachal means 'the hill of the teeth' and the next mountain is called 'Tooth Mountain'. It seems that the English sappers got their nomenclature a little garbled when they were surveying in the nineteenth century. Considering this imprint the latter mountain seems the better candidate for the dental title.

3 *The Rabach*
The ruined village in the upper reaches of Cummeengeera, which never had a road into it, illustrates the lengths to which people had to go to find a modicum of cultivatable land in pre-famine Ireland.

There is a macabre story of a double murderer, Sean an Rabach, who dwelt here. He killed an Englishman, probably a deserter from a ship in Berehaven, and strangled a woman

The ruined village in Cummeengeera

who found out about this crime. Many years later he was caught and hanged, the last person in the province to be executed, it is said.

4   *The Earth Ringfort*

This earth ringfort is one of the tens of thousands scattered all over Ireland and dating from about 2000 BC to AD 500, though some date from much later and a few were inhabited until 1700. Homesteads were built within them and the fort acted as a shelter from the wind, and a protection at night for cattle against wolves, etc. They seldom had any direct military significance (see p. 15).

149

Map 2.27 :
Mullaghanattin

2·27

MULLAGHANATTIN

Mullaghanattin is sometimes called the Matterhorn of Kerry; from many angles this peak, in the centre of the mountainous Iveragh Peninsula, displays in miniature the same proud triangular profile of the famed Swiss Alp. This route, with Mullaghanattin as its centrepiece, is a high-level circuit round a secluded basin appropriately called the Pocket. There is therefore little possibility of navigational error, these errors being more probable in finding the start! Nonetheless, as you gaze initially around at the horseshoe looming above, you might be forgiven for doubting if you are in the right place. Mullaghanattin is straight ahead along the line of the incoming road but it scarcely appears to rise above the horizon line. Patience! The pyramid emerges into full view as you traverse the circuit, along with an unexpected bonus: the first sight of the tangle of mountains west of Cloon Lough — bare, grotesquely distorted rock strata and tiny lochans one above the other — is a spectacle to remember.

ROUTE DESCRIPTION (Map 2.27)

Walk onwards for 300 yards (270 m) to a gate, and beyond it turn R beside a fence. Follow the fence steeply uphill through crags. Mercifully the steepness soon relents, yielding to a more gentle slope of short grass. At the fence junction near the crest of the hill swing L with the line of fencing that you have followed thus far, and where it eventually veers R downhill continue along the bumpy ridge taking in some steep but avoidable crags among the first of the bumps (they are hard to enumerate exactly).

    Walk along the high broad ridge to enjoy easy terrain and good views of the nearby Reeks to the north-east and the even nearer Lough Brin *(1)*. At a small, circular, flat and grassy mound — an unexpected feature hereabouts — turn west, i.e. to the L, to face the increasingly impressive cone of Mullaghanattin. First drop to a very narrow gap and then climb steeply with cliffs R all the way to the OS obelisk marking the summit *(2)* (2539 ft/773 m).

    Continue west steeply downhill from the summit to a fearsome gully on the R (do not take it!). Just beyond this on higher ground look out for the simple plaque to Noel Lynch *(3)*. Ascend

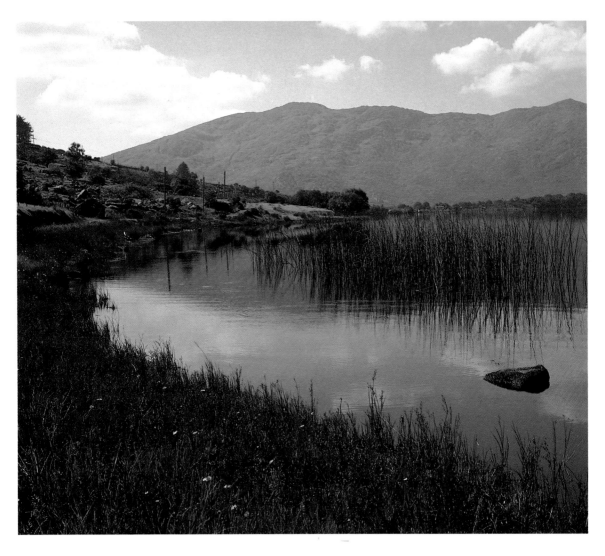

Mullaghanattin from Lough Brin

further along the ridge to Beounn (2468 ft/752 m), which is not named on the maps. It is the highest point on a very narrow grassy ridge giving truly spectacular views to the west of Cloon Lough, an amazing tangle of bare rock and lonely lochans.

From Beounn descend south to a pass and climb from there to a broad, rounded peak simply labelled 639 m on the 1:50 000 map. Continue south-east from point 639 m, so dropping towards the corner of the Pocket and crossing diagonally a series of sandstone slabs which further slow down already slow progress. At the valley floor pick up a rough track, turn R and follow it to an impressive group of farm buildings. Ask permission to go through the farmyard (it will be readily given) and continue along the track to a metalled road. Turn L here, cross two bridges and you will reach the parking area at the (relatively) main road.

The Pocket

1 *Monster at Lough Brin*
   This lake is reputed to harbour a Loch Ness type monster; it is only one of a number of Kerry lakes to make such a claim. However, the evidence is a lot more slight than for the Scottish monster.

2 *Rainfall in Kerry*
   A few miles north-east of here at Ballaghbeama Gap the greatest annual total rainfall (156 inches/3965 mm) was recorded. A few miles north-west (Coomacarrea) is the area that had the greatest monthly total (27 inches/686 mm) — a rather unenviable propinquity!

3 *Plaque to Noel Lynch*
   This plaque commemorates a Dublin man, an international climber who was killed in a simple walking accident in 1973. The sentence translates as 'The Blessings of God on his soul'.

3·28

TRAILS AROUND
KILLARNEY

STARTING AND FINISHING
POINTS
Start at the car-park of Muckross
House (970861) which is well
signposted. From Killarney take
the N71 (Kenmare road) for
about $3\frac{1}{2}$ miles (5.5 km) turning R
here for the House. The short
route also finishes here. The long
route ends at Kate Kearney's
Cottage (881887), which is also
well signposted. Take the
R562/T67 (Killorglin road) from
Killarney turning L after $5\frac{1}{2}$ miles
(9 km) and follow the signs for the
cottage.
MAPS
This walk is covered by a variety
of OS and other maps at 1:50 000
and one-inch to the mile scales.
The recommended map is the OS
1:25 000 Killarney National Park
(scheduled for 1992).
LENGTH
The short route is $14\frac{1}{2}$ miles
(23 km) long but this can be
shortened to 7 miles (11 km) if a
car is available at Derrycunihy
church (914803). The long route
is also $14\frac{1}{2}$ miles (23 km) long.
ASCENT
1050 ft (320 m) for the short
route; 1750 ft (530 m) for the
long.

Killarney is sickly-sweet famous, the subject of scores of maudlin
songs and tasteless ballads. This type of tourist shrine is usually
best avoided as the reality all too often fails to live up to expecta-
tion. Nevertheless, Killarney, or rather the area around, does
not disappoint: it is a spectacular interplay of woods, lakes and
mountains.

Two routes are described here, both following the Old Kenmare Road. They start at Muckross House and climb by Torc
Waterfall before settling down to paths over moorland and
through oakwood in an area that is one of the last fastnesses of the
Irish red deer. One route returns towards Killarney along the
Kerry Way, and gives good views of Muckross Lake and its
wooded shores. This we call the 'short route' in the following
text, though it actually only involves less climbing.

Alternatively, one can continue away from Killarney on the
Kerry Way, descend to the shores of the Upper Lake and from
there climb the awesome cleft of the Gap of Dunloe with
towering cliffs to right and left to end at Kate Kearney's Cottage
near Killarney. This we call the 'long route'.

ROUTE DESCRIPTION (Map 3.28)

From the car-park walk round the R of the House (1), to meet the
Kerry Way (2), which should be followed until otherwise indicated. Take the driveway west (3) and then south with the shore of
Muckross Lake on the R and the heavily wooded Torc Mountain
ahead. Continue along the driveway through woodlands and take
the tunnel at a clearing on the R under the N71.

On the other side of the road a steep climb ensues alongside
the cascade below Torc Waterfall, the climb's severity only
partly disguised by dense vegetation. At the T-junction towards
the top, turn L to gain a car-park, this evidence of motorized
ascent being a rather annoying revelation in the light of recent
efforts. Here is the start of the tracked section of the Old Kenmare Road (4).

The Upper Lake, Killarney

Take the forest road south-west passing the forest bar, cross a bridge and turn L immediately afterwards to walk through a pleasant oakwood. Less than a $\frac{1}{2}$ mile (0.8 km) further on pass a gate which has a notice explaining that one is entering the terrain of the red deer *(5)*, and listing certain misdeeds that one is emphatically not to perpetrate. No need to specify: responsible walkers would not dream of committing them.

The forest road continues steadily upwards to the south-west, shrinking to a narrow path at the Crinnagh River, where planks form several rudimentary bridges. If in doubt a little further on, keep between the low Cores Cascade on the L and a quaking bog on the R and head for a few oak trees sheltered by massive slabs.

The path resumes faintly beyond the oaks, passing to the L of further slabs *(6)*. Ascend gradually to the crest of the hill, beyond

NOTE
Dogs are strictly forbidden in the deer country through which these routes run.

155

which pass to the R of a ruin (the first prominent ruin). From here on, old sessile oaks dominate with green moss growing luxuriantly on tree trunk, ground and rocks alike in profusion, stimulated by warmth and high humidity. At the clear track beyond this wood, turn R and walk down to the N71 at Derrycunihy church. At this point there is a choice of route.

Short route Assuming no car pick-up here, one can take the short route back to Muckross. Leaving the Kerry Way turn R along the N71 and walk down the road for $4\frac{1}{2}$ miles (7 km) to the sign for Dinis, a road giving enchanting views of Muckross Lake and the mountains beyond. Turn L here to follow a narrow, metalled road over peninsulas between Muckross Lake and Lough Leane all the way back to Muckross House.

Long route Alternatively, one can tackle the long route. Turn L on the N71, walk 100 yards (90 m) along the road, then go R at the walking-man signpost to follow a path down through woods. This stretch of path is marked by indicators — posts or paint spots — every few yards, and all are needed given the errant path's perverse tendency to shake off walkers. The path ends at a signpost near a ruin. Turn L here to follow a well-mannered path which runs round the end of the Upper Lake and leads eventually to Gearhameen, where the tower of a lime kiln and a lovely old stone bridge herald a road.

Turn L at the T-junction beyond the bridge (a waymark would be useful here) and continue on the road through pastoral land past Black Valley Youth Hostel and thence to the hamlet of Black Valley beyond.

The next task is to penetrate the great wall of mountains to the north (R): easily described, less easily done. Turn R steeply uphill in the hamlet onto a rough but motorable track (thus leaving the Kerry Way) and climb to the Gap of Dunloe, whose high point is at the near end, 450 ft (140 m) above and only $1\frac{1}{4}$ miles (2 km) away by road. Once there, the full magnitude of the Gap *(7)* becomes apparent, a deep defile cut between the Purple Mountain group to the east (R) and the Reeks to the west (L).

From the high point of the pass take the road on a slow but steady descent past four lakes and into a gradually widening valley all the way to Kate Kearney's Cottage. The slow physical descent is matched by a slow descent into mundaneness; jaunting cars *(8)* and day-trippers become more frequent and all sense of isolation eventually disappears. However, as you await your lift at the cottage, sipping a beverage in comfort, you may conclude that the mundane aspects of life bring some small but welcome comforts in their train.

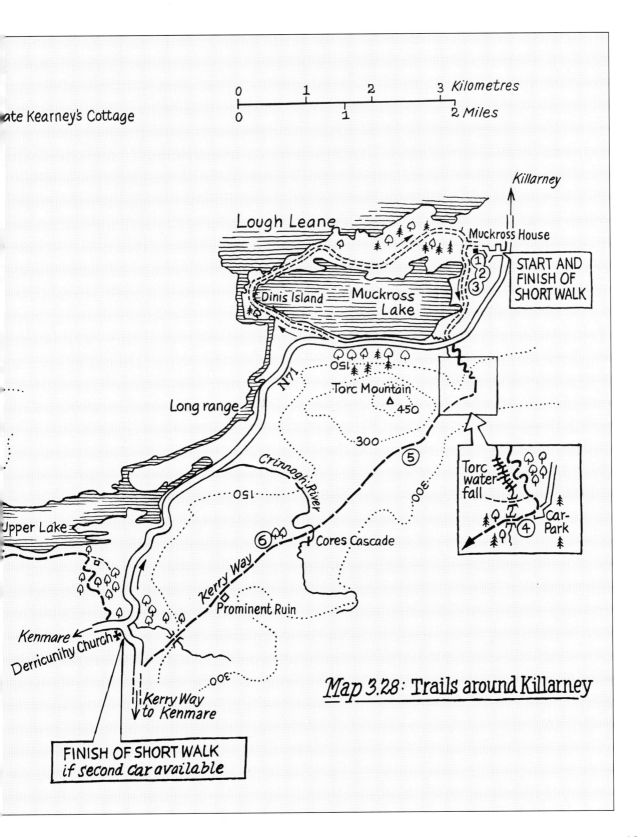

ate Kearney's Cottage

0   1   2   3 *Kilometres*

0   1   2 *Miles*

Killarney

Lough Leane

Muckross House

① ② ③

START AND FINISH OF SHORT WALK

Dinis Island

Muckross Lake

N71

OSI

Torc Mountain
△ 450

Long range

300

⑤

Torc water fall

Car-Park

Ⅰ ④

300

Crinnagh River

150

Upper Lake

⑥

Cores Cascade

Kerry Way

Prominent Ruin

Kenmare

Derricunihy Church

Kerry Way to Kenmare

Map 3.28: Trails around Killarney

FINISH OF SHORT WALK *if second car available*

300

157

1 *Muckross House and Killarney National Park*

The House was completed in 1843 in the Elizabethan style. It lay vacant for a number of years prior to 1964, when it was opened to the public as a museum of Kerry folk life. This museum still flourishes and there is now an audio-visual display illustrating the environment of the National Park. The gardens are informal with large expanses of lawn fronting magnificent vistas of lake and mountain.

Killarney National Park covers 25,000 acres (10,000 hectares) and is the largest designated park in Ireland. It takes in the area west and south of Killarney, encompassing a wide variety of mountain and lake habitats. On its south-western edge it includes the summit of Mangerton Mountain; its western edge runs parallel and close to the Gap of Dunloe (see note 7 below).

2 *The Kerry Way*

The Kerry Way is shaped like the frame of a tennis racket. The 'handle' runs from Killarney south-west to near Derrycunihy church, where it forms a loop which runs right round the Iveragh Peninsula. The total distance is 135 miles (215 km), thus making it the longest of the Republic's Long Distance Routes. Wherever possible, it follows paths and unsurfaced roads with only a few linking stretches of metalled road. Since it runs generally higher than the motor roads, the views, already excellent from these, are even further enhanced.

3 *Kerry Cattle*

The grazing area here is for a pedigree herd of Kerry cattle. At one time the dominant breed of cattle in Ireland, these sturdy cattle have been largely confined to Kerry for the last 200 years.

4 *The Old Kenmare Road*

This was the main road between Killarney and Kenmare until the 1840s when it was closed by the local landowners who wanted the land for deer-hunting rather than farming. There are still remains of tillage, ruins and field boundaries along the route, testimony to the unfortunates who were so summarily driven from their homes.

5 *Red Deer*

The red deer of Killarney, numbering about 350–400, are the only deer of any kind in Ireland of native stock, all others being introduced. The main herd roams the moorlands and mountain slopes around here and towards Mangerton to the east. The smaller but more numerous sika deer live mainly in the woodlands. The deer are particularly impressive during the rutting season in October.

6   *The Napoleonic Peace in Ireland*
    Nineteenth-century graffiti adorns the sandstone slabs here,
    the most prominent of which reads in a neat script: 'James
    Neill Tippy Regt 1815' ('Tippy' is short for 'Tipperary').
    Exactly why James Neill had time to pursue such peaceful
    pastimes in rural Ireland while Europe was at war is not
    known.

7   *The Gap of Dunloe*
    This great U-shaped gash 1500 ft (460 m) deep is a glacial
    breach formed from a major regional ice-sheet centred
    around Kenmare to the south. The glacier emanating from it
    pushed northwards, gouging out the Gap to reach the plains
    around Killarney.

8   *Jaunting Cars and Jarveys*
    The jarveys of Killarney, the drivers of the jaunting cars,
    have been habitually described in Victorian guide books as a
    band of cut-throat, ruthless mercenaries who would sell
    their grannies for a quick profit. You will have to judge for
    yourself whether the Victorians underestimated their black-
    guardism!

The Reeks from the Kerry Way

3·29

THE COOMLOUGHRA HORSESHOE

STARTING AND FINISHING POINT

At the junction of the unclassified road running along the north-west side of Lough Acoose with that running along the eastern side (759859). Assuming that one is facing uphill on the main street in Killorglin take the road signposted Cappanalea on the L of this street. After 0.8 miles (1.3 km) fork R, also signposted Cappanalea, and continue ahead for another 6.8 miles (10.9 km). The exact parking place is not critical and you may wish to drive the car a few hundred yards up the road along the eastern side of the lake, thus shortening the walk at both ends.

MAPS

This walk is well covered by a variety of OS and other maps at 1:50 000 and one-inch to the mile scales. The recommended map is the OS 1:25 000 'The Macgillycuddy's Reeks'.

LENGTH

6½ miles (10.5 km)

ASCENT

4050 ft (1240 m)

The sharp arête of the Beenkeragh Ridge is the finest in Ireland, falling in stretches sheer to the east and almost as steeply to the west. At its south stands Carrauntoohil (pronounced *Carawn-too-hill*) at 3414 ft (1039 m) the highest peak in Ireland; to its north is Beenkeragh, only 100 ft (29 m) lower and the second highest mountain. Beyond these proud and stately peaks the ridge sweeps in one direction to Skegmore and in the other to twin-peaked Caher (pronounced *Care*), the third highest. All these peaks and the fine ridges between them surround the hour-glass shaped lakes of Coomloughra and Eagher. This is by far the finest ridge walk in Ireland and many would say the most exhilarating and rewarding circuit.

ROUTE DESCRIPTION (Map 3.29)

Walk a ½ mile (800 m) down the minor road along the eastern side of Lough Acoose, turning L off it opposite a prominent headland of Lough Acoose to cross rough, pathless ground and meet a fence and path parallel to it running along the north-west spur of Caher. Turn R here and follow the path and fence over good ground. Where the fence ends continue upwards still on a clear path through a boulder field to attain the first of the two peaks on Caher, which inexplicably has two adjacent cairns. The main top, which has to make do with one cairn, is a little farther on. At 3200 ft (975 m) it predictably commands marvellous views. Cliffs fall steeply L into Coomloughra, Carrauntoohil rises ahead and to its L the jagged Beenkeragh Ridge terminates in the great rocky mound of Beenkeragh. Among the many peaks to the west the pyramid of Mullaghanattin is the most prominent.

   Still on a clear path follow the narrow ridge east of Caher. From the col towards Carrauntoohil take the broad boulder-strewn ridge to the summit itself by-passing, near the summit, the Beenkeragh Ridge on the L. On this ascent, note the long ridge running east. This is the eastern section of the Reeks *(1)*, a fine arc of mountains which boasts no fewer than three or five

SAFETY NOTE

The route, mostly a narrow ridge, is easy to negotiate navigationally, as the many cliffs in the area do not allow much latitude for error. If you suffer from *severe* vertigo do not attempt the ridge from Carrauntoohil to Beenkeragh (the 'Beenkeragh Ridge'), especially if the rocks are likely to be wet or if winds are high. The walk is in an anti-clockwise direction: this allows the highest peak in Ireland, Carrauntoohil, to be climbed *before* the Beenkeragh Ridge, so that one will at least have had the satisfaction of achieving this if one has to retreat. An anti-clockwise circuit also means that the difficult stretch of the Beenkeragh Ridge (it is near Carrauntoohil) is tackled early on thus facilitating a return if necessary.

Monros (it depends what is considered a Munro as there is not much of a drop between some of them).

Carrauntoohil (3414 ft/1039 m) is crowned by an ugly cross, a cairn and an OS obelisk *(2)*. Its summit stands as a promontory squarely facing north, looking over the plains of Kerry beyond the Hag's Glen. The views encompass much of what has already been described on the ascent and so need not be repeated. Among the many mountain features visible the formidable, steeper side of the Beenkeragh Ridge undulating jaggedly near at hand must attract what is hoped is a not too nervous eye.

So to the Ridge. Retrace your steps to the south-west for 100 yards (90 m), and then descend directly and steeply to the Ridge, which runs initially north-west (*Important: it is suicidal to attempt to walk directly to the Ridge from the summit of Carrauntoohil*). Once on the Ridge the crux, a rocky gendarme, comes early. The vertigo-free will clamber over the airy summit, the rest will scramble ignominiously lower down on the L. After this, the rest of the Ridge can be enjoyed as there is nothing half so scaring ahead. Now that *some* relaxation is possible (but not too much, carelessness can still easily result in disaster), watch out particularly for the Hag's Teeth far down on the R, great prongs of rock in the glen of the same name.

Beenkeragh is reached after a short, steep, rocky ascent. At 3314 ft (1010 m) it is the only mountain in Ireland besides

The Beenkeragh Ridge from Caher

Carrauntoohil to attain 1000 m. The views are magnificent, especially back towards Carrauntoohil. After Beenkeragh take the ridge heading north-west (not the one north-east) towards Skregmore (2790 ft/850 m) and if this is done correctly, navigation thereafter is simple; the ground, steep on both sides, is ample warning against carelessness and the only possible error is the gross one of wandering down the subsidiary ridge towards Skregbeg.

Map 3.29 : Coomloughra Horseshoe

Skregmore is, for the theoretically minded anyway, a problem. The five tops are difficult to distinguish, having only three cairns between them. For the record, the third of these tops, the one from which a ridge heads to Skregbeg, is the highest. Skregbeg is useful to the academics for determining exact positions — while the rest of us get on with the job of climbing all the tops.

There is likely to be no mistake about the descent from the 'fifth' Skregmore: its steepness has an air of finality. From its foot, head for the mouth of the long narrow Lough Eighter (not to be confused with Lough Eagher to the east). Take the rough road *(3)* at the mouth for the short distance to the bridge, and leave it here to follow the L bank of the river downstream. After 500 yards (450 m) where the river bends sharply R, veer southwest over a boggy saddle between rocky outcrops. Beyond these, head to the R side of the prominent headland mentioned in the first paragraph of the route description to reach the road. Turn R for the starting point.

1   *The Reeks*

The Reeks (properly the Macgillicuddy's Reeks — so named after a former local landlord) stretches from the Gap of Dunloe and runs all the way to and including Skregmore. The Munros and Tops (doubtful Munros), starting at the Gap of Dunloe and working west, are: Cruach Mhor (3062 ft/ 933 m), an unnamed top, Knocknapeasta (3190 ft/973 m), an unnamed top, Cnoc an Chuillin (3141 ft/958 m), Carrauntoohil and Beenkeragh (3314 ft/1010 m). The Reeks Walk, an annual long distance walk starting at the northern end of the Gap of Dunloe, took in all the peaks to Carrauntoohil and ended at Lough Acoose. It was discontinued in recent years partly because of the erosion caused by too many walkers.

2   *Carrauntoohil*

At 3414 ft (1039 m) this is the highest mountain in Ireland, though only the third of the four highest mountains in each of the countries in the British Isles. The bicycle which unaccountably used to be suspended on a bar at the summit has equally unaccountably disappeared.

Isaac Weld, an early mountaineer writing in 1807, used only barometric observations estimated the height of the mountain at 3418 ft, a remarkably accurate figure. He gives a vivid account of a direct descent from the summit of 'Gheraun-tuel' (as he spells it), one which cannot be recommended:

We were conducted to a precipice, at least sixty feet deep, down which we were told it was necessary to take our course. The proposal startled us, nor did we consider how it

Lough Acoose and the Reeks

was practicable; but the guide seating himself at the brink of it, on a rock which presented an even surface nearly to the bottom of the precipice, slid down it, taking the precaution, however, to impede the velocity of the descent, by catching hold of the tufts of long grass which grew from the crevices at either side. His example was followed without hesitation.

3 *Hydro Scheme at Lough Eighter*
This scheme is funded as a Valorean EC project. It generates a minute amount of electricity in a country which already has an ample supply. The approach road, which is all too evident, is a brutal intrusion in an area of great beauty. Two pipes run from here: a 6-inch one for Killorglin water supply and an 18-inch one for the generation at Cottoner's River.

BRANDON

The church (on the L) in the
village of Cloghnane (511114).
From Tralee take the R559/T68
and then the R560 following signs
for Brandon or Brandon Point.
The village itself is rather
indifferently signposted, and to
make it worse the Gaelic form
'Cloghan' is used in places along
the road.
MAP
OS half-inch to the mile Sheet 20
covers the area, but very
inadequately. (OS 1:50 000 Sheet
70 is scheduled for 1991.)
LENGTH
11½ miles (18.5 km)
ASCENT
4000 ft (1210 m)

At least one Scotsman has declared Brandon to be the finest
mountain in the British Isles. While the not-so-canny Hamish
Brown may now regret what might have been a hasty, off-the-
cuff-remark (let's be charitable to the disloyal Scot), Brandon is
undoubtedly a superb mountain. Far out towards the western end
of the Dingle Peninsula, its eastern side plunges in a series of
corries and cliffs to Brandon Bay, to inert boglands and to the
high Conor Pass. West and north it confronts the Atlantic in a
sweep of sea-cliff broken by isolated coves. A unique delight is
the chain of paternoster lakes, a dozen or so (it depends on what
you count as a lake) perched one over the next. These are set into
the long corrie which truncates the summits of both Brandon and
Brandon Peak, its high southern extension. The route described
is probably the finest traverse of the mountain, offering marvellous scenic views on a safe, not-too-long circuit with, unusually
for this part of the world, a clear path at least as far as the
summit.

ROUTE DESCRIPTION (Map 4.30)

With the church on the L, walk past a plaque to airmen lost in
World War II *(1)*, on the R of the village street. Turn L onto a side
road after ½ mile (0.8 km) from the start (it is signposted 'Hill-
crest'), walk uphill to the T-junction, turn L and at the upper end
of a severe S-bend where the road ends at a farmhouse, follow
two signposts encouragingly labelled 'Mt Brandon'. This is the
start of the Pilgrims' Route.

The second signpost leads to a grotto near at hand from where
a path, needlessly adorned with obtrusive red and white poles,
leads gradually uphill with higher ground on the R. At a large
cairn (the first) the views, up to this point dominated by Brandon
Peak and only slowly varying, open up dramatically. The paternoster lakes *(2)* are revealed one by one, and as the path swings R
it faces directly into the head of the corrie, cliffs rising jaggedly
and menacingly in nearly all directions.

Keeping to the path *(3)*, pass a lochan (four close together will
be visible from higher up) and ascend the corrie wall on a steep
but safe path. At the corrie top, turn L and with the sheer drop

Map 4.30 : Brandon

Labels on map: Grotto · STARTING AND FINISHING POINT · Cloghnane · Tralee · Brandon (4) · (3) · (2) · L.Nalacken · L.Cruttia · Brandon Peak · Gearhane · L.Avoonane · 750 · 600 · 450 · 300 · 150 · N

| 0 | | 1 | | 2 | | 3 Kilometres |
| 0 | | | 1 | | | 2 Miles |

into the corrie L, walk 350 yards (320 m) to Brandon (3127 ft/953 m) *(4)*. The views from the summit are varied: dominated by the ocean to the north and west, and by plain and mountain in other directions. It is a wonderful panorama — when it can be seen — for Brandon is often cloud-topped, or as they say in the neighbourhood — 'it mostly wears its cap'.

South of Brandon the path disappears, but no matter since all that is needed is to keep the corrie cliffs on the L and walk downhill (except for one short rise) all the way to the col towards Brandon Peak. In bad weather, the col may be recognized by a wall which meanders in from the R across the slope near the col, and abdicates to a line of stones at the col itself. South of the col climb steadily, cliffs still on the L, to cairned Brandon Peak (2764 ft/842 m).

The Paternoster Lakes

From the Peak continue south on a gently undulating slope to Gearhane, a short narrow ridge about 2250 ft (685 m) high with steep grassy slopes on both sides. Walk down the gentle slope south of Gearhane on what is now a spur to an upland gate, flanked by fences at an unusually acute angle. Keep to the L of the fences and the gate so keeping close to the steep ground on the L.

Follow the spur as it swings L and gently descends, a descent which postpones and exacerbates the inevitable — a short but tough, steep descent through high heather. On this descent veer L to a sheep dip on the road to avoid new forestry directly below the nose. Gain the road at the dip and walk $2\frac{1}{2}$ miles (4 km) back to the village, turning L at the outskirts of the village to reach the church.

167

The Blaskets from Brandon

1 *The Plaque in Cloghnane*

The plaque commemorates the Polish, British and German airmen who died in four separate plane crashes, all of which occurred in the area in the years 1940–43. One of the crashes occurred on the hill to the R of the Pilgrims' Route. Another crash in those years was that of a German fighter plane which landed with little damage. The crew set it on fire before it could be impounded.

2 *Paternoster Lakes*

The paternoster lakes are so called because the chain resembles the beads on a rosary, one of whose prayers is the 'Our Father' (*Pater Noster*). Some authorities claim that there are 16 lakes in the chain.

3 *St Patrick's Cabbage*

St Patrick's Cabbage (*Saxifraga spathularis*) grows freely in the rock crevices here. The flowers, which are open from May to July, are pink and white with crimson spots; the leaves grow in a basal rosette and are narrow towards the base. It is prolific among the mainly acid rocks of Cork and Kerry. London Pride is a hybrid of it.

4 *Brendan the Navigator*

The mountain is named after St Brendan the Navigator, who set sail from Brandon Creek near here in about the year 550 with a band of fellow monks, and who (apocryphally) discovered Greenland and even America. It is accepted that Iceland and probably Greenland were colonized from Ireland before the arrival of the Vikings, so the hagiography has some basis. The unimpressive mounds of stones on the summit are termed St Brendan's Well and Oratory.

In 1868 an amazing 20,000 people attended a mass here.

APPENDICES
Access and Rights-of-Way for the Walker

Particularly in the Republic, but also in Northern Ireland, there is a great discrepancy between the strictly legal situation on rights-of-way and public access and the practical situation. *Legally*, in both jurisdictions hillwalkers have right of passage only in National Parks, on Long Distance Routes and in some state forests. In addition, in Northern Ireland there is a modest system of rights-of-way along the lines of those in England and Wales. In practice, however, in both jurisdictions the situation is much more favourable than this.

If a walker is in open (i.e., unenclosed) country he has little to fear and is much more likely to be exchanging greetings rather than trading insults with the farmers he encounters. In enclosed fields and near farmhouses it would be prudent to seek permission to cross land or walk through farmyards, and it is unlikely that a polite request will be refused. In this context the closing off of commonage (see p. 16) at present a minor but growing threat, makes access considerably harder.

Of course, the walker can expect a less than civil reception if he is not following the Country Code. To the farming community, the two most important items of this Code (but not the only ones) relate to dogs and fences.

Dogs must be under proper control, particularly in sheep country — and most of the uplands are sheep country. Walkers should never stand on fence wires; they may look the same afterwards but they are in fact irretrievably weakened. In a few places on these walks fences are to be crossed. However, there are gaps in most fences, and where there are not, there are always convenient rocks to facilitate a crossing.

Walkers enjoy this live-and-let-live attitude everywhere in the uplands. The only possible exception is Wicklow, which is so near a large city and its hordes of vandals that some farmers' tempers have understandably become somewhat frayed. The routes given in this book for Wicklow should not result in clashes. Elsewhere in Wicklow and, of course, in the contiguous mountains of County Dublin, one should be circumspect and heed notices.

It has to be admitted that, especially for visitors, this situation is not completely satisfactory. A visitor used to cast-iron rights-of-ways may, at least initially, feel uneasy in a country of goodwill but no guarantees. A few forays should improve their confidence; after all, it is supposed to be Ireland of the welcomes!

Safety

Safety is a dull topic — until an emergency when the effects of not taking safety measures will be suddenly and powerfully evident. Do not postpone sensible precautions until it is too late.

Of all the factors influencing safety, weather is the most important by far. The easiest route in bad weather can be far more hazardous than the hardest one in good weather. Cloud, wind and rain disorientate, weaken and chill, as well as drastically reducing your enjoyment. In cloud it is easy to veer by 180° in a few minutes when you think that you are walking straight ahead.

Other variables are the area and how well you know it, the number of people on the walk and their abilities, the quality of available maps (a severe handicap in the Republic), the time to darkness and the severity of the route. For instance, in good weather with a small, strong party, in an area you know well you can try a far more strenuous route than you would try if all these factors were unfavourable. In any event, an experienced party in bad or changeable weather should always consist of at least four people.

The route you walk and the precautions you take will depend on the variables listed above, always remembering that in Ireland the hills are likely to be unfrequented and a mountain rescue service may take a long time to reach the scene of an accident.

Before you set out, therefore, in a spirit of fine, careless rapture you should refer to the following checklist, all items of which should be carefully considered.

Before you go
Listen to the weather forecast.
Choose a route appropriate to your experience and the weather.
Leave a note of your intended route.

Take with you
A basic first aid kit, sufficient food and drink, proper clothing (especially boots) with some as spare, a small torch in winter, map and compass (the latter is particularly important in Ireland). Leave a change of clothing in your car.

On the walk
Keep an eye on deteriorating conditions and turn back if these warrant it — if you think you can just about make it, don't try.
Keep clear of cliffs, especially in high winds.

If an accident occurs
Keep calm. Keep the patient as warm and comfortable as possible and then go for help with a note of the injuries and the patient's exact position. Mountain rescue may be alerted, north or south, by ringing 999 and asking for mountain rescue.

Lastly, at all times take with you a few cells of commonsensical grey matter between your ears. They are your best guarantee against disaster.

Giving a Grid Reference

A grid reference is an excellent way of 'pinpointing' a feature, such as a church or mountain summit, and can be determined from all Ordnance Survey and most other maps mentioned in this book.

Grid lines, which are used for this purpose, are shown on these maps. They are the thin lines one kilometre apart drawn vertically and horizontally on the map thus producing a network of small squares. Each line, whether vertical or horizontal, is given a number from 00 to 99, with the sequence repeating itself every 100 lines. The 00 lines are slightly thicker than the others thus producing large squares each side representing 100 km and made up of 100 small squares. Each of these large squares is identified by a letter. The entire network of lines covering the island of Ireland is called the National Grid.

The left-hand diagram shows a corner of a map which contains a Youth Hostel. Using this map, the method of determining a grid reference is as follows:

Step 1

Holding the map in the normal upright position, note the number of the 'vertical' grid line to the left of the hostel. This is 72.

Step 2

Now imagine that the space between this grid line and the adjacent one to the right of the hostel is divided into ten equal divisions (the right-hand diagram does this for you). Estimate the number of these 'tenths' that the hostel lies to the right of the left-hand grid line. This is 8. Add this to the number found in Step 1 to make 728.

Step 3

Note the number of the grid line below the hostel and add it on to the number obtained above. This is 21, so that the number becomes 72821.

Step 4

Repeat Step 2 for the space containing the hostel, but now in a vertical direction. The final number to be added is 5, making 728215. This is called a six-figure grid reference. This will enable the Youth Hostel to be found on *any* map on which the National Grid is drawn.

A full grid reference will also include the identification of the appropriate 100 kilometre square of the National Grid; for example, R728215. This information is given on each map.

Maps for the Walker

The present position on maps for walkers is quite complicated. Because the recommended map or maps is given for each walk within the text, it is more appropriate here to concentrate on the advantages and disadvantages of the various series and to give the coverage, which is patchy and in any case changing rapidly, only in very general terms.

Northern Ireland

A good 1:50 000 layer-tinted series with 10 m contour intervals covers the entire area and a few neighbouring parts of the Republic. It shows paths, forests and cliffs accurately, and although the colouring is in places laid on with a heavy hand so that it can be difficult to read contours on the hills, these maps are generally excellent.

A 1:25 000 map covers the Mournes; it is in the same series as the excellent British series. One disadvantage of this map is that its large size makes it hardly suitable for refolding in high winds on a mountainside, which its large scale makes necessary frequently.

The other relevant Northern Ireland series is the half-inch to the mile (1:126 720), which is useful not because of its coverage of Northern Ireland, but because it covers large areas of the north of the Republic not covered so well by the Republic's maps.

The Republic
Here the situation might be described as an uncertain dawn after a long dark night.

The whole state is covered by a half-inch to the mile (1:126 720) series with100 ft contour intervals. The series is none too accurate: forests are vaguely indicated; roads and paths tend to be out of date; and cliffs are indicated, but are so patchy and inaccurate that the symbols are of limited value. Where there is a choice, the half-inch Northern series should be used as it is much superior, not least in presentation. It is hardly necessary to add that the scale is far too small. For instance, to represent the 48 sq miles (12,500 hectares) of the complex tangle of peaks, ridges and valleys of the Twelve Bens on a baggage-label-sized 12 sq in (80 sq cm) is clearly grossly inadequate.

Four areas, three of which are of interest to walkers, are covered by the 'District' one-inch to the mile (1:63 360) series. The maps in this series are layer-tinted and have a 100 ft contour interval to 1000 ft and 250 ft above 1000 ft — hence they give the impression that Irish mountains are gently sloped in their higher reaches. Paths are shown except for the very significant omission of the Long Distance Routes. Perhaps it might be more accurate to say that they are shown as they were 100 years ago. Cliffs are badly and inaccurately depicted. Forests are clearly depicted but are not always up to date; inexplicably, forest tracks are usually highly inaccurate. In general this series is barely adequate, and the contouring in particular is poor. It should also be noted that only a small proportion of the mountain area is covered.

The latest series to appear is by far the best, but only a few sheets are at present available and even these are labelled 'preliminary'. This series, on a scale of 1:50 000, is not layer-tinted, but is accurately contoured with 10 m intervals, the latter a huge attraction to the mountaineer. Cliffs are not explicitly depicted and have to be judged solely by the convergence of contour lines, which are never omitted no matter how close they are. Paths are not adequately shown (except some Long Distance Routes) and the depiction of forests may be out of date, but these are comparatively minor matters. This series is recommended for the areas — at present small areas — which it covers. The Ordnance Survey hope to cover the entire state at 1:50 000 and to cover some mountain areas at 1:25 000 by 1998–99. They expect that two at the latter scale covering some of the mountains of the south-west will be available in 1992.

Finally, one special-purpose series and one privately produced map should be mentioned; other maps of specific areas are covered as they occur in the walk descriptions. The special-purpose series is that published by the Office of Public Works and is available at National Park centres. The series covers the small National Parks and surrounding areas on a scale of one-inch to the mile (1:63 360) with 100 ft contour intervals, and with cliffs roughly indicated (one of the series, Glendalough is at 1:25 000 with a 15 m contour interval). The series is quite reliable and up to date. The paper is flimsy, but since the maps cost only a few pence each this does not matter too much, unless the map disintegrates in pouring rain on an unknown mountainside — as tends to happen.

A private firm, Folding Landscapes, Roundstone, Co. Galway, has published a map (and guide) to Connemara on a scale of 1:50 000 with a 30 m contour interval and cliffs accurately depicted. Unfortunately, the paper is very flimsy. However, the map shows paths, forests and placenames accurately and comprehensively. Placenames are shown in the original Gaelic form, not the anglicized versions recorded by English surveyors in the nineteenth century (see p. 20).

For the walks covered by the Connemara map this has led to a problem: whether to use the mangled but well-known anglicized versions or the 'correct' but little-known Gaelic ones. Both versions are given at the first mention and thereafter sions are given at the first mention and thereafter

the anglicized. The OS has not yet finalized which version it will adopt for the new 1:50 000 series.

At the moment the Connemara map is the best available in the south and almost as good as those in the north.

Addresses of Useful Organizations

Republic of Ireland

An Oige — Youth Hostel Association of
Ireland,
39 Mountjoy Square,
Dublin 1
Dublin (01) 363111

An Taisce — National Trust for Ireland,
Tailors Hall,
Back Lane,
Dublin 8
Dublin (01) 544794

Association for Adventure Sports,
House of Sport,
Longmile Road,
Dublin 12
Dublin (01) 509845

Bord Failte Eireann — Irish Tourist
Board,
Baggot Street Bridge,
Dublin 2
Dublin (01) 765871

Coillte Teoranta — Irish Forestry Board,
Leeson Lane,
Dublin 2
Dublin (01) 615666

Conservation Volunteers Ireland,
Royal Dublin Society,
Dublin 4
Dublin (01) 681228

Cospoir — The National Sports Council
Hawkins House,
Hawkins Street,
Dublin 2,
Dublin (01) 734700
(responsible for Long Distance Routes)

Irish Peatland Conservation Council,
3 Lower Mount Street,
Dublin 2
Dublin (01) 616645

Irish Wildbird Conservancy,
Ruttledge House,
8 Longford Place,
Monkstown,
Co Dublin
Dublin (01) 2804322

Irish Wildlife Federation,
132a East Wall Road,
Dublin 3
Dublin (01) 366821

Mountaineering Council of Ireland,
House of Sport,
Longmile Road,
Dublin 12
Dublin (01) 509845

Office of Public Works,
51 St Stephens Green,
Dublin 2
Dublin (01) 613111
(OPW is responsible for National Parks)

Ordnance Survey of Ireland,
Phoenix Park,
Dublin 8
Dublin (01) 213171

Northern Ireland

Conservation Volunteers (Northern
Ireland),
The Pavilion,
Cherryfield Playing Fields,
Ravenhill Road,
Belfast BT6 0BZ
Belfast (0232) 645169

Department of the Environment,
Conservation Service,
Calvert House,
23 Castle Place,
Belfast BT1 1FY
Belfast (0232) 230560

National Trust,
Regional Office,
Rowallane House,
Saintfield BT24 7LH
Belfast (0238) 510721

Northern Ireland Tourist Board,
River House,
48 High Street,
Belfast BT1 2DS
Belfast (4) 246609

Ordnance Survey of Northern Ireland,
Colby House,
Stranmillis,
Belfast BT9 5BJ
Belfast (4) 661244

Royal Society for the Protection of Birds,
Belvoir Forest,
Belvoir Park,
Belfast BT8 4QT
Belfast (4) 491547

Sports Council for Northern Ireland,
House of Sport,
Upper Malone Road,
Belfast BT9 5LA
Belfast (4) 381222
(Responsible for Long Distance Routes)

Youth Hostel Association of Northern
Ireland,
56 Bradbury Place,
Belfast BT7 1RU
Belfast (4) 324733

INDEX

Achill Head, 104–7
Achill Island, 97
Adair, John George, 68
Aghla Beg, 91, 92
Aghla Mor, 91, 92
Allenwood Power Station, 35
Altan Lough, 92
Altnagaighera, 108, 109
An Chailleach, 131
An Uillinn Thair, 116
Annalong Valley, 54
Ardnageer, 86, 87
Art's Lough, 59
Astelleen Waterfall, 66

Ballinclea Bog, 63
Ballyteige Castle, 32, 35
Bealick, 138
Beara Peninsula, 146
Bearnagh, 45, 54
Bearnagh Crags, 45
Beenacouma, 135
Beenkeragh, 160–2, 163
Beenkeragh Ridge, 160–1
Belmullet, 104
Ben Bulbin, 78–81
Ben Crom Reservoir, 57
Ben Lettery, 126, 128, 131
Ben Lugmore, 123
Benbaun, 126
Benbreen, 126, 128
Benbury, 122
Benchoonas, 108–11
Bencollaghduff, 126
Bencorr, 126
Bencullagh, 131
Benglenisky, 128, 131
Bengower, 128
Bennaunmore, 142–5
Beounn, 152
Bingorms, 65
Binn Bhan, 127
Binn Bhraoin, 126, 128
Binn Briocain, 117–19
Binn Chorr, 126
Binn Dhoir Chlair, 126
Binn Dhubh, 126
Binn Fhraoigh, 108
Binn Gabhar, 108
Binn Ghleann Uisce, 128
Binn Leitri, 126
Bireca, 147
Black Valley, 156
Blaskets, 135, 137
Bloody Foreland, 74
Blue Stacks, 64, 86–9
Boycott, Captain, 107

Brandon, 132, 165–9
Brandon Peak, 165–7
Brandy Pad, 56, 57
Brendan, St, 169
Brown, Hamish, 165
Bundorragha River, 124
Burren, 113–15
Burtonport, 95

Caher, 160
Caher River, 115
Caheranardurrish, 115
Caherdoonfergus, 113, 115
Camaderry, 43
Camarahill, 58
Camenabologue, 59
Cappagh Glen, 144, 145
Carrauntoohil, 160–1, 163
Cecil Newman Memorial, 47
Clare, 96
Clifden, 96
Cloghnane, 169
Cloghoge House, 25
Cloghoge Valley, 27–31
Cloon Lough, 152
Cnoc an Chuillin, 163
Cnoc na hUillean, 116
Comeraghs, 25, 36–9
Commedagh, 56
Connemara, 26
Connemara National Park, 128, 131
Conor Pass, 165
Coomacloghane, 146–7
Coomloughra, 132, 160–3
Corabber River, 88
Cores Cascade, 155
Coumalocha, 39
Coumfea, 36, 39
Coumshingaun, 39
Cove Mountain, 54
Crinnagh River, 155
Croagh Patrick, 97, 105
Croaghgorm, 87
Croaghnamaddy, 74
Croaghaun Mountain, 104–5
Crocknalaragagh, 92
Cruach Mhor, 163
Cumeennahillan, 146
Cummeengeera, 146–9
Curraghreague, 148
Cush, 51

Daingean, 135
Dereen Tropical Gardens, 148
Derricunihy Church, 156
Derrybeg Bog, 68
Derryclare, 126

Derryveagh Mountains, 65, 70
Devil's Coachroad, 56
Dingle Peninsula, 132, 134, 165
Dobhach Bhrainin, 113
Donegal, 64, 86
Doo Lough, 121–2, 124
Drumcliff Church, 80
Duaghruagh, 108
Duchruach, 108
Duncap Isle, 74
Dunlewy, 82, 84
Dunlewy Lough, 82
Dunmore Head, 135
Dunquin, 137

East Town, 77
Errigal, 65, 82, 90–5
Eskatarriff, 147

Failmore Valley, 116
Finbar, St, 140, 144
Fofanny Reservoir, 45, 47
Foilastookeen, 138
Fox, Arthur, 84

Galtees, 51
Galtybeg, 51
Galtymore, 25, 50–3
Galway, 96
Gap of Dunloe, 154, 159, 163
Garraun, 110
Gearhane, 167
Giant's Causeway, 145
Gleann Eidhneach, 128
Glen of Imaal, 25
Glen River, 56
Glencar, 78
Glencoaghan, 126–31
Glendalough, 25, 40–4
Glenealo, 40, 44
Glengarriff, 152
Gleninagh, 113–15, 128
Glenmalure, 59, 63
Glenveagh, 65, 66–9
Glenveagh Castle, 66
Glenveagh National Park, 67, 82
Glover, Joey, 91, 93
Gougane Barra, 134, 138–42
Gougane Barra Lake, 139
Great Blasket, 135, 137
Great Skelligs, 135

Hag's Teeth, 161
Hare's Gap, 45
Horn Head, 65, 74–7
Hungry Hill, 147

Illion West, 116
Inishnabro, 135
Inishtooskert, 135
Inishvickillane, 135
Iveragh Peninsula, 151

Kavanagh's Gap, 61
Keem Bay, 104–6
Kerry, 132
Kerry Way, 154, 156, 158
Kildare, 32–6
Killarney, 134, 154–9
Killarney National Park, 158
Killary Fiord, 100
Killary Harbour, 96, 98–103, 122
Knocknacloghoge, 27, 29
Knocknahillion, 116
Knocknapeasta, 163
Knocknaveachal, 146, 148
Kylemore Abbey and Chapel, 108, 111
Kylemore Lough, 110–11

Lackbane, 148
Lake Crohane, 142, 143, 144
Leitrim Mountain, 61, 64
Letterbreckaun, 117–19
Letterfrack, 131
Letterkenny, 95
Letterkenny and Burtonport Extension
    Railway, 95
Little Killary Harbour, 100
Little Skelligs, 135
Little Slaney River, 58
Lobawn, 61
Lough Acoose, 160
Lough Aluirg, 92
Lough Barra, 65
Lough Barra Bog, 72
Lough Beg, 82
Lough Belshade, 86, 89
Lough Brin, 151, 153
Lough Curra, 51–2
Lough Dan, 27–30
Lough Diheen, 51, 52–3
Lough Eagher, 160, 163
Lough Eighter, 163
Lough Eske, 88
Lough Glas, 138
Lough Guitane, 142, 144
Lough Gulladuff, 87
Lough Inagh, 126

Lough Maumbeg, 82
Lough na Crapai, 109
Lough Nabroda, 142
Lough Nambrackderg, 138
Lough Slievesnaght, 70
Lough Slievesnaghtbeg, 71
Lough Veagh, 66, 68
Louisburgh, 124
Lowtown Marina, 32, 33
Lugduffs, 25, 40–4
Luggala, 27, 30
Luggala House, 30
Lugnaquillia, 25, 43, 58–63
Lullymore Bog, 35
Lynch, Noel, 151, 153

Maamturks, 96, 98, 116–19
Maamturks Walk, 120
Macgillicuddy's Reeks, 138, 151, 160,
    163
Mackoght, 92
Mam na bhFonsai, 127
Mam Eidheach, 128
Mam Ochoige, 116
Mangerton, 144
Maumina, 128
Maumlack, 82
Mayo, 96
Meacanach, 131
Meelbeg, 47, 48
Meelmore, 45, 48
Mount Eagle, 134, 135–7
Mourne Wall, 45, 48, 54, 56
Mournes, 26, 54–7
Moyteoge Head, 104, 105
Muckanaght, 131
Muckish, 65, 74
Muckish Gap, 91, 92, 93
Muckross House, 154, 158
Mullaghanattin, 132–3, 151–3
Mweelrea, 97, 98, 108, 121–5

Newby, Eric, 107
Newcastle, 56
Newman, Cecil, 47

Old Kenmare Road, 154, 158
Otway, Caesar, 95, 131
Owenglin River, 128

Paps, 138

Poisoned Glen, 65, 82–5

Rabach, Sean an, 148
Robertstown, 26, 32
Roc, Saint, 102
Rocky Cap Mountain, 70–1, 84
Rosguill, 74
Roughty River, 143

Salrock Church, 102
Sayers, Peig, 137
Sgilloge Lough, 36–7
Sheep Haven, 74
Shehy Mountains, 138
Silent Valley, 45, 54, 57
Skegmore, 160
Skregbeg, 162–3
Slieve Bearnagh, 26, 45–9
Slieve Binnian, 26, 54
Slieve Commedagh, 56
Slieve Donard, 26, 56
Slieve League, 64
Slieve Meelmore, 45
Slieve Snaght, 65, 70–3, 84
Slievelamagan, 54
Slievenaglogh, 45
Sligo, 64
Spink, 41–3
Sugarloaf, 61

Table Mountain, 61
Tearaght, 135
Tonelagee, 59
Tooth Mountain, 146, 148
Torc Mountain, 154
Torc Waterfall, 154
Tory Island, 77
Traglisk Point, 74
Twelve Bens, 96, 126

Uggool, 102
Ulster Way, 45, 47, 48, 86, 88

Weld, Isaac, 163
Western Way, 119
Wicklow, 25
Wicklow National Park, 25, 44
Wittgenstein, Ludwig, 100

Yeats, W. B., 78, 80